contemporary lace making

contemporary lace making

constance nieuwhoff

VAN NOSTRAND REINHOLD COMPANY
New York Cincinnati Toronto London Melbourne

Van Nostrand Reinhold Company Regional
Offices: New York Cincinnati Chicago Millbrae Dallas

Van Nostrand Reinhold Company
International Offices:
London Toronto Melbourne

Library of Congress Catalog Card Number 74-6794
ISBN 0-442-30071-9

Translated from the Dutch by Danielle Adkinson

Photography by Henk Beukers
Line drawings by Annet Spruyt

Printed in the Netherlands

Published by Van Nostrand Reinhold Company,
450 West 33rd Street, New York, N.Y. 10001
and Van Nostrand Reinhold Company Ltd.,
Molly Millar's Lane, Wokingham, Berks.

16 15 14 13 12 11 10 9 8 7 6 5 4 3 2 1

Library of Congress Cataloging in Publication Data
Nieuwhoff, Constance.
Contemporary lace making.
Translation of Vrij kantklossen.
Bibliography: p.
1. Lace and lace making. I. Title.
TT800.N513   746.2'2   74-6794
ISBN 0-442-30071-9

Contents

Captions to colour plates

Plate 1: (facing page 24): Handspun linen, dyed with cold water dyes (left); handspun wool, dyed with plant dyes (right).

Plate 2: (preceding page 25): Four examples of a lace garland.

Plate 3: (facing page 40): 'Dancing figures'.

Plate 4: (preceding page 41): Three-dimensional lace.

Plate 5: (facing page 48): 'Embryo'.

Plate 6: (preceding page 49): Three examples of the 'Thorn apple' design.

Plate 7: (facing page 56): 'Moss'.

Plate 8: (preceding page 57): 'Mussel shell'.

Introduction

1. FOREWORD

Lace is basically a gauze-like weave which is made by braiding or knotting loose threads, to create open and closed areas in a complete pattern. Crochet hooks, knitting needles, and bobbins can be used in the process. There are only two basic movements in lace making: turning and crossing.

Bobbin lace is, as the name implies, lace made with the aid of bobbins. It is essentially a form of plaiting, perfected in Europe in the 16th and 17th centuries, and the finished work looks like the traditional idea of lace — a fine, white weave, remarkable for its great intricacy. The stitches of most of the lace meshes from all over the world are similar to those found in the finest bobbin lace of the 17th century.

Bobbin lace can in fact be made from a variety of materials, and does not necessarily have to be fine and white. Most of the designs shown in this book are an attempt to take a new look at lace by combining a traditional technique with modern ideas of texture, form, and colour.

This book discusses, step by step, the ways of making lace with bobbins, and shows the reader the correct tools and how to use them. Once the basic techniques of bobbin lace have been mastered, unique, individual shapes and textures, fine or coarse, can be designed and created. The book is intended for people who want to express their own creativity in lace making, and who do not want the restrictions and limitations of a set design or pattern.

2. A SHORT HISTORY OF BOBBIN LACE

Man used to satisfy his need for food by killing a bear or other wild animal. The skins of the animals were used to provide warm clothing; sometimes they were used to sleep on, or stitched together to form a shelter. When man abandoned his nomadic habits and began to settle in one place, he started to cultivate the land and to domesticate animals for various purposes. It gradually became obvious that, as the animals bred, it was good economics to live off the surplus ones. Man also realized that he could use the coats of certain animals without killing them first.

It was probably noticed that sheep often left tufts of fleece in bushes as they passed; these were then collected, and primitive man made his first attempts at imitating the sheep's coat. The first weaves were perhaps made of small branches, grass, and stray lengths of animal hair, intertwined like reeds.

Then, by overlapping and twisting a number of short animal hairs, it was seen that a thread could be created. This process could be facilitated by using a small stick, stone, or bone. The wool was tied to the stick or stone, then drawn out and twisted. It was thus discovered that it was possible to make threads of considerable length. Spinning had been invented.

The discovery of a means of making longer threads meant that man could also envisage making much larger weaves. This led in due course to the invention of the first weaving loom, which in Europe consisted of two uprights linked by a crossboard, round which the threads were passed. The ends of the threads were weighted with stones, and the weft thread was woven under and over. The threads used in this method of weaving, known as far back as the Stone Age, were always left long at each end of the weave. These loose ends were then plaited and knotted to provide an additional decorative element in weaves destined to be made into clothes or blankets. Braiding could be made easier by tying small pieces of wood to these lengths of thread; in this way, bobbin lace and macramé techniques came to be invented.

This led ultimately to the making of lace from loose threads. The actual method of plaiting, however, remained unchanged; it still consisted of turning and crossing actions, and, whatever the country of origin of the lace, these two basic elements are always found.

Like many other traditional crafts and skills, then, bobbin lace making has developed from very basic techniques — from simple plaiting of loose threads with primitive tools to the intricate white lace seen in old paintings and museum collections.

During the 17th and 18th centuries, bobbin lace making began to develop into a cottage industry in most European countries. The lace was made for personal use — for the decoration of household linen and clothing.

Lace is usually judged on its technical and visual merits, both of which were extremely high in this period. However the circumstances in which this beautiful lace was produced, and the living conditions of the craftsmen, were unmentionable. The lace makers of Flanders, for instance, were often tied for life by contract to the lace merchants, who provided the craftsmen with tools and materials, and then purchased the finished lace for sums which were barely sufficient to ensure survival.

The material used in the manufacture of the very fine Flemish lace was linen, which is easiest to work with when kept damp; for this reason the lace makers were forced to work in damp cellars, devoid of sunlight and fresh air, which meant that tuberculosis was rife among them.

In the guise of charity, the Church and the merchants combined to found 'schools' for the daughters of the poor. In return for meagre board and lodging in appalling conditions the girls were taught how to make lace to satisfy the requirements of the aristocracy, the Church, and the prosperous bourgeoisie. Apprenticeship started at the age of five, and a girl was supposed to be capable of providing for herself by the time she had reached ten.

It is occasion for sober reflection, when we look at the fine examples of 17th century lace, and think in what circumstances they were made for the adornment of the privileged few. We should not forget that these beautiful objects are the products of exploitation.

Fig. 1: Collection of the Nordiska Museet, Stockholm

1

2

Equipment and materials

1. TRADITIONAL EQUIPMENT AND MATERIALS FOR MAKING BOBBIN LACE

During the 16th century, the basic equipment was a large pillow, stuffed with sawdust, seaweed, horse-hair, or straw, and covered with a strong linen cloth. The bobbins were made from pieces of wood and were so shaped that the thread could not slide off the wood. There were no set patterns available, and such as there were simply passed from mother to daughter. Sometimes lace was secured during its making with wooden pegs, the forerunner of pinning.

Later, when lace making had become a more commercial, as well as a more refined and laborious, enterprise, more sophisticated tools were needed. It was now that patterns first began to appear; they were made from stiff paper in which holes were punctured where the lace was to be secured (Fig. 2).

A round or oval pillow is used in modern lace making; some pillows incorporate a revolving cylinder, which is useful when long sections of lace are being made. Bobbins are made from palm, birch, or olive wood, depending on the country and the pattern being followed.

In England, the bobbins were often decorated with beads of various colours and shapes; they served a dual purpose, making it easier to remember the point reached in the work, and helping to weight the bobbins, so that the threads were always well stretched.

In Fig. 3 on page 10, the following basic equipment is illustrated: (1) a bobbin lace pillow with rotating cylinder, stuffed with horse-hair and seaweed; (2) a reel for winding the bobbins (not absolutely necessary); (3) brass pins (brass is essential because it is rustproof; stainless steel pins can be used, but the steel must be of very high quality indeed); a variety of bobbins from (4) Belgium, (5) Sweden, (6) England, and (7) Spain; (8) bobbin lace yarn (very strong linen yarn consisting of two or three intertwined threads, obtainable bleached or unbleached); (9) graph paper for drawing lace patterns.

2. EQUIPMENT AND MATERIALS
FOR CREATIVE BOBBIN LACE

Some of the tools and materials mentioned above can also be used for creative bobbin lace, especially when first learning the technique of making lace with bobbins.

A round flat pillow is required, with a diameter of about 24 ins. (58 cm.), and about 2 ins. (4.8 cm.) thick in the centre; this can either be purchased, or specially made by an upholsterer.

The back consists of a wooden disc. The pillow is stuffed with sawdust, which is covered with a thin layer of plastic foam, and finished off with upholstery material. The material is fastened round its circumference to the disc by a strip of plywood about $\frac{1}{2}$ in. (12 mm.) thick (see Fig. 4).

A leather handle is attached to the back of the pillow to make it easier to carry around. A strong cotton cover is also very useful for protecting the unfinished work on the pillow. The cover is made from a circle of strong cotton material about 33 ins. (80 cm.) in diameter. It should be hemmed all round the edge, and then a piece of elastic should be passed through the hem and pulled tight until the cover fits snugly over the pillow.

Some long brass pins are required, also drawing paper and a child's exercise book with pages ruled in $\frac{1}{4}$ in. (6 mm.) squares. The first designs are worked with quite thick yarn, which is why smaller squares cannot be used.

About 30 bobbins are needed to begin with. If the thread is fairly thick, make sure that the bobbins are not too small. Making bobbins is discussed on page 12.

Instead of the pillow described above, a piece of cork measuring at least 16 ins. × 24 ins. (39 cm. × 58 cm.) can be used, but this is really only suitable for lace makers with some experience, who want to produce larger, more ambitious works. A sheet of paper can be fastened round the cork with staples or Sellotape. The pattern is then drawn on the paper.

In theory, practically any yarn can be used: even human hair has sometimes been used! In the 19th century lace bracelets and necklaces were made from human hair. These were intended as keepsakes, in the same spirit as the antique lockets in which people used to put locks of hair.

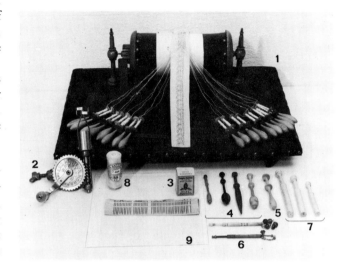

3

4

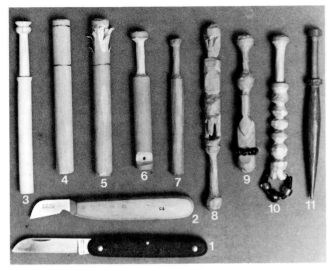

5

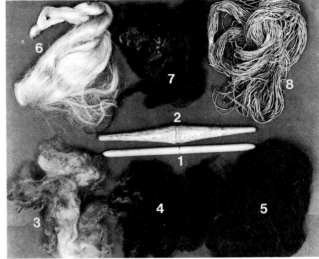

6

Fig. 5:
1: penknife or pruning knife
2: wooden carving knife
3: Spanish bobbin
4: stage 1
5: stage 2
6-11: home-made bobbins, plain and decorated

Fig. 6:
1: simple distaff
2: more complex distaff
3, 4: rough white and brown sheep's wool
5: handspun sheep's wool
6: unspun flax
7: unspun dyed flax
8: spun and dyed flax

7

Fig. 7:

Various materials that can be used in making bobbin lace:

1: single ply weaving wool
2: 2 ply weaving wool
3: single ply handspun sheep's wool
4: single ply linen (no. 14/1)
5: single ply handspun flax
6: twisted linen thread (no. 3/2)
7: single ply sisal string
8: 2 ply jute string
9: copper wire, 0.5 mm.
10: 2 ply knitting cotton
11: 2 ply mercerised cotton

The traditional yarn used for lace making is white 2 ply linen yarn, which is usually smooth and very strong. A high quality flax, with very long, fine fibres, is needed to produce a suitable quality of linen yarn. Since lace is often used as a collar, or to embellish underwear, it has to be washable. Because linen fibres are strong, the lace will remain taut when removed from the cushion. In the 16th century, gold and silver yarn were used in lace making, as well as coloured and black silk yarn.

Linen yarn is by far the best for beginners; it does not have to be very white or very thin at this stage. It is the easiest type of yarn to work with because it is very smooth. If a fairly thick linen yarn is selected, it will be easier to see whether the work is being done correctly or not. A 6/2 or 8/2 yarn are probably the most suitable thicknesses; the figure before the stroke indicates the thickness of the yarn (the higher the figure, the thinner the yarn), and the figure after indicates the number of threads forming the ply. When a little experience has been gained, all sorts of other materials can be experimented with: single ply untwisted linen yarn of varying thickness; single ply handspun sheep's wool; single ply handspun linen (see the section on spinning with a distaff); single ply or 2 ply wool — preferably weaving wool which does not stretch; even string, buttonhole silk, raffia, thin copper and iron wire, and ribbon can be used (see Fig. 7).

3. HOME-MADE TOOLS

Bobbins can of course be bought ready-made, but they can also be made quite easily. A very sharp knife is required, or a small saw, and a length of wooden rod about $\frac{3}{4}$ in. (18 mm.) in diameter. Pine cuts very easily, but any kind of wood can be used, providing that it is soft and does not splinter. The quantity of wood depends on how many bobbins are required — allow about 6 ins. (15 cm.) per bobbin. These instructions are for a bobbin based on a Spanish model.

The rod should be cut into lengths about $5\frac{1}{2}$ ins. (12 cm.) long. At about $\frac{1}{5}$ in. (5 mm.) and $1\frac{1}{5}$ ins. (3.5 cm.) from the end of the rod, a line should be drawn round the wood. A groove is then cut along these lines. Then, starting from the upper groove and moving downwards, the wood should be cut away round the circumference of the rod. It should not be cut higher than about $\frac{3}{4}$ in. (18 mm.) from the top. Then the process is reversed and the wood is cut away upwards, starting from the lower groove. The section between the two grooves becomes the neck of the bobbin, round which the thread is to be wound. The wood should be whittled down until the neck measures about $\frac{1}{5}$ in. (5 mm.) in diameter. The bobbin should be cut as carefully as possible, and finally smoothed down with sandpaper. It is now complete in all essentials.

If decoration is required, the lower part of the bobbin can be carved. If a hole is bored through the wood about $\frac{1}{5}$ in. (5 mm.) from the bottom end, a length of copper wire can be passed through it, and threaded with beads as the English lace makers used to do. Before attempting this, however, an experimental hole should be bored in a waste piece of the wood, to make sure that it does not splinter too easily.

Fig. 5 on page 11 shows the various stages in the development of the bobbin, as described above; some of them are so heavily carved that they look like miniature totem poles!

The pillow and the bobbins are ready, and some consideration should now be given to the materials that are to be used. These, too, can be produced oneself, if

12

8

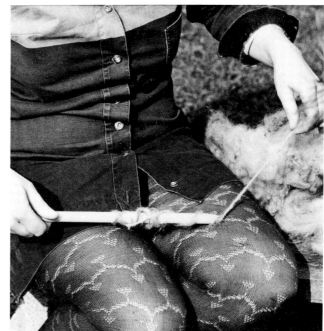

9

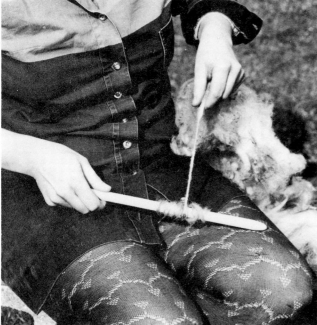

10

11

desired. A short length of wood and some rough sheep's wool or flax will be required.

In the introductory section, the likely process was described by which our ancestors came to discover how to pull out rough sheep's wool, and to make it into a thread by twisting. The way to do this with the help of a short piece of wood is described below.

This little distaff can be made from a length of wooden rod about $\frac{3}{5}$ in. (15 mm.) in diameter, and about 12 in. (29 cm.) long. Both ends should be cut or filed down to a fairly blunt point. In the middle of the rod a groove is cut all the way round, to secure the ends of the thread when starting off (Fig. 6, no. 1). Anyone skilled in wood-work could make a more elaborate distaff, about 2 ins. (4.8 cm.) in diameter in the middle, which tails off to points at either end (Fig. 7, no. 2). This kind of distaff is heavier, and will make the work go faster.

4. SPINNING WITH A DISTAFF

A length of any thin, soft yarn about 10 ins. (24 cm.) in length is fixed in the middle of the distaff. This short length of yarn will help to start off the main yarn. A handful of rough, unwashed sheep's wool is now unravelled — it should be pulled *in the opposite direction to that of the wool fibres* until there is a good-sized bunch of loosened fibre. It should not be pulled too hard, since the unravelled fibre must not be pulled completely away from the main part of the wool.

The distaff is held in the right hand and placed on the upper part of the left thigh (or the reverse for left-handed people) (Fig. 8). The thread, together with a portion of the unravelled wool fibre, should now be taken between the thumb and index finger of the left hand. The distaff should then be turned to the right with the right hand; at the same time the length of thin yarn is allowed to slip off the point of the distaff, which should form an angle of 120° with the yarn (Fig. 9).

It will soon be noticed that the wool between the left thumb and index finger is also beginning to turn. This process is coninued until the starting yarn and the wool have begun to form one single thread. A length of the yarn can now be wound on to the distaff by changing the angle between it and the thread to 90° (Fig. 10). The

distaff is then placed on one's lap, and another handful of wool pulled apart with both hands, again taking great care that the unravelled wool does not become completely detached from the main part (Fig. 11). The length of yarn which is turned at any one time by the action of the distaff can be exactly determined: the portion of wool to form the yarn is held tightly between thumb and index finger about 12 ins. (29 cm.) from the point of the distaff, and this is the only length of wool which should be allowed to turn. The distaff is once again turned to the right, until this new handful of wool has become a good-sized length of yarn, which can then be wound on to the distaff again. These actions are repeated until sufficient yarn has been spun.

If the wool is turned too much, it will become twisted and start to curl, so this should be avoided.

Linen yarn is made in exactly the same way. A piece of flax is pulled apart against the direction of the fibres, so that these, which are going to be spun, can be seen clearly.

Yarn made in this way can be twisted together to form multiple ply yarn, which is stronger and thicker. Two balls of spun flax or wool are required. A thread from each ball is knotted to a piece of string, which is in turn fixed to the distaff.

The two threads are taken in the left hand, and the distaff is turned to the left with the right hand. It will soon be seen that the two threads, which were spun originally by turning the distaff to the right, are starting to twist together. The threads that are being twisted together should not be too long at any one time, otherwise the ply yarn will lose its smoothness and become over-twisted. When a length of 2 ply yarn has been prepared, it can be wound on to the distaff; then the next pair of threads to be twisted is taken up between the thumb and index finger of the left hand.

Having provided one's own yarn, it is of course perfectly possible to dye it oneself as well. This is not in fact very difficult, and the processes are described in the next three sections. There are two basic ways of dyeing yarn — with chemical dyes or with plant dyes.

5. DYEING WITH COLD WATER DYES

Dylon Cold or Procion M will dye most kinds of absorbent natural fibre. The manufacturer's instructions should always be read very carefully before using the dye. This kind of dye should not really be used for wool since it does not mix with albumen.

Unspun flax or spun linen yarn can be dyed in 45 minutes. If dyeing unspun flax, it is advisable to use high quality flax with fine fibres. The dye penetrates these fine fibres very slowly, producing a variety of shades as the flax dries. If an evenly dyed yarn is preferred, it is better to spin the yarn first and dye it later.

About $\frac{1}{5}$ oz. (5 g.) of dye is needed for every $\frac{1}{5}$ lb. (100 g.) of material to be dyed — in other words, about $\frac{4}{5}$ oz. to 1 lb. Dyes can be mixed to obtain a particular colour effect: green added to yellow, for instance, gives a beautiful apple green, while a touch of orange added to purple gives a warm reddish violet.

Methods and times vary slightly between different brands of dyes, but general instructions are given here for dyeing 100 g. of flax. Metric quantities only are given, to avoid unwieldy fractions.

Five g. of the chosen dye is disolved in the correct amount of lukewarm water (follow the manufacturer's instructions) in a jug or old saucepan. (Rubber gloves should be worn when handling dyes.) This mixture is then poured into a plastic bucket containing enough cold water to cover the flax, which is first dampened, and then placed in the dye mixture. The flax fibres should be manipulated and pulled apart in the dye. After the flax has soaked for about 15 minutes, about 200 g. of salt should be stirred into the dye bath. After another 15 minutes, 100 g. of soda should be stirred in, which helps to fix the dye into the flax. After another 15 minutes, the flax is ready for rinsing. It should then be wrung out and dried; when quite dry, it can be spun into yarn using a distaff. The dyed mass of flax may look rather unwieldy, but if pulled out a little by hand, it will spin quite easily.

The dye bath can be used again, though it may be necessary to add a little more salt and soda; the second lot of flax will be a slightly lighter shade than the first.

The dye bath can be used over a period of about four hours, after which time the dye tends to lose its strength.

6. DYEING WITH INSTANT DYES

All kinds of materials can be dyed with these dyes, with the exception of certain synthetics such as Acrilan and Orlon (again, read the manufacturer's instructions). Eight g. of dye (Dylon, Rit, and Drummer are some of the best known brands) is needed per 100 g. of yarn. Colours can be mixed, if desired. Basically, the method of using instant dyes is as follows. The appropriate quantity of dye is dissolved in hot water. This mixture is brought to the boil, and a tablespoonful of salt added. Sufficient warm water is added to cover the yarn completely; the dye bath is then heated to about 40ºC. The wet yarn is placed in the bath, which is then heated up to 80º-100ºC.

The bath must remain at this temperature for about 30 minutes. The yarn is then rinsed once in hot water, once in lukewarm water, and then hung up to dry. This method of dyeing is clearly both simple and rapid. Many shades of the same colour can be produced by dyeing different materials in the same dye bath (wool, linen, cotton, and hemp, for example). As each material absorbs a different amount of dye, no two shades will be the same. It is in fact very useful to have a large assortment of yarn available when beginning to make free bobbin lace.

7. USING PLANT DYES FOR WOOL

In the last two sections, dyeing wool, linen, and other materials with chemical dyes was discussed. However, many of the examples of lace illustrated in this book were made from woollen yarn dyed with plant dyes. To have spun one's own yarn, and possibly even collected the basic material, if it is sheep's wool, surely merits taking a little extra trouble to prepare one's own dyes as well. Indeed what could be more natural than using the only kind of dyes known up to 1850 — dyes made from vegetable matter? Chemical dyes have only existed for 100 years, while plants have been used for 4000! Plant dyes used on wool yield very beautiful colours; indeed, the dyes and material go so well together that it seems a pity to go to the expense of buying chemical dyes, when chestnut leaves, perhaps even from one's own garden, produce the most exquisite effects.

Recipes can be found for hundreds of plants which can be used in dyeing. There are, for instance, dozens of recipes for dyeing material yellow or brown. Since a large number of plants produce similar colours, something suitable will almost certainly be found close at hand.

Some species of plants are already very rare, and these should not be picked, since they stand little enough chance of survival. Indeed, they may actually be protected by law. Autumn leaves make very good dyes, and it is no trouble to pick up leaves that have already fallen to the ground.

One simple recipe for plant dyeing is given below, together with instructions on following it. Anyone wanting to do a lot of plant dyeing would find it worthwhile to obtain a specialist book on the subject.

It is best to use handspun, 100% wool yarn. Cotton and linen are more difficult to dye with plant dyes. Spun wool should be washed in fairly warm water containing soap powder, then rinsed in tepid water and hung out to dry. It should not be spun dry.

Before the wool and plants are put together to boil, the wool should be treated with mineral salts; those most commonly used are alum, and potassium bichromate; both can be obtained from a chemist, or specially ordered if necessary. As the mineral salts dissolve, they open up the scales of the wool fibres so that the fibres can be more easily penetrated by the dye. The salts also help to fix the dye in the wool fibres, and to give a stronger colour, using fewer plants. The colours will also be much more fast when the wool has been pre-treated. Alum (usually 15%) gives lighter colours, while potassium bichromate (usually 3%) gives duller, faded colours. These salts, when used in dyeing, are known as mordants.

When using fresh plants, they should weigh six times (i.e. 600%) the weight of the wool; if using dried plants, use twice (i.e. 200%) the weight of the wool. All quantities below are given as percentages of weight; in other

16

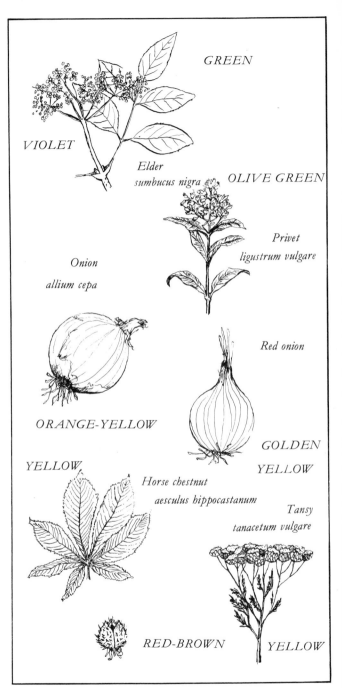

GREEN

VIOLET

Elder
sumbucus nigra

OLIVE GREEN

Privet
ligustrum vulgare

Onion
allium cepa

Red onion

ORANGE-YELLOW

GOLDEN
YELLOW

YELLOW

Horse chestnut
aesculus hippocastanum

Tansy
tanacetum vulgare

RED-BROWN

YELLOW

12

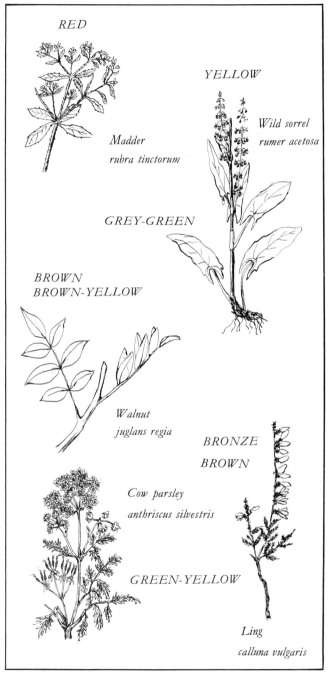

RED

Madder
rubra tinctorum

YELLOW

Wild sorrel
rumer acetosa

GREY-GREEN

BROWN
BROWN-YELLOW

Walnut
juglans regia

BRONZE

BROWN

Cow parsley
anthriscus silvestris

GREEN-YELLOW

Ling
calluna vulgaris

13

words, the quantity of dry wool is given as 100%, whatever its actual weight.

Taking a specific example: 200 g. of wool is to be dyed a golden yellow, using heather. The wool is first treated with 15% of its weight in alum. The following amount of alum is therefore required: 100% of the wool is 200 g., 1% of which is 2 g.; 15% is $15 \times 2 = 30$ g. This quantity of alum is dissolved in hot water in an old saucepan, then poured into an enamel or copper bucket or kettle. As much water as is needed to cover 200 g. of wool is then added.

The wool which is to be dyed must first be thoroughly soaked for 15 minutes in lukewarm water. The mineral salt solution (alum and water) is then heated to about 40ºC.; the wet wool is placed in the solution, which is then brought to the boil. It should boil for one and a half hours before the wool is removed.

The weight of heather required is 600% of the weight of the wool, in other words 1200 g. in this instance. When the wool has been pre-treated with alum, the 1200 g. of heather should be placed in another bucket with some water, and heated to 40ºC. The treated wool is placed in this bath, which is brought to the boil. It should then be left to boil for two hours. The wool should be left to cool in the dye bath, and finally rinsed in lukewarm water. After rinsing, it should be hung up to dry. If there are any ticks in the wet wool, wait until it is dry before trying to remove them.

A plant dye bath can often be used a second or third time (perhaps with madder, cochineal, or walnut), preferably again with pre-treated wool. When treated with alum, wool does not have to be rinsed before dyeing, but it must be rinsed if treated with potassium bichromate.

The colours of the handspun wool used for the examples of bobbin lace in this book can all be obtained by following the above general instructions, using various plant dye recipes.

PLANT	PART USED	MORDANT	COLOUR	REMARKS
logwood	bark	15% alum 3% pot. bichromate	blue purple	
cochineal (chemist)	powder 10%	15% alum 3% pot. bichromate	cyclamen pink light purple strong	add salt to water
turmeric (chemist, food shops)	powder 5%	15% alum	yellow	not very fast; second bath with madder gives a strong orange
cow parsley	whole plant	15% alum	green-yellow	
heather	whole plant (cut above ground)	15% alum 3% pot. bichromate	gold-yellow bronze brown	
chestnut	leaves, shells, or husks	15% alum 3% pot. bichromate	yellow red-brown	
privet	small branches with leaves	3% pot. bichromate	olive green	
madder (chemist)	powder 10%	15% alum 3% pot. bichromate	bright red dark red	
onion (yellow)	skin	15% alum	orange-yellow	
onion (red)	whole onion, in sections	15% alum 3% pot. bichromate	gold-yellow bronze yellow	
elderberry	leaves berries	15% alum 3% pot. bichromate	green violet	
	berries	15% alum	lilac	
walnut	leaves husks	15% alum none	brown-yellow brown	
sorrel	whole plant	15% alum	grey-green	

14   *gauze stitch*

15   *cloth stitch*

16   *rose-net*

17   *plaiting*

The technique of making bobbin lace

1. INTRODUCTION

The following sections deal with the actual making of bobbin lace, but one or two patterns are included as a guide. The work is easy at first, and becomes more difficult later. After reading the first two sections, it should be possible, even at this early stage, to produce some lace. It is best to start with the first pattern, rather than choosing a later one that seems more attractive; otherwise some important technical term or explanation may be missed.

The creative lace making further on in the book will offer no real problems once the basic techniques of bobbin lace making have been mastered.

2. THE STITCHES

Lace making with bobbins is based on two simple actions: turning and crossing the threads.

Bobbin lace is always made with pairs of bobbins, in other words two bobbins are used together. Sometimes they remain together throughout the whole of the work; sometimes one or both are used independently before coming together again.

When adjacent threads are passed round each other it is called 'turning'; *in turning, the right-hand thread is always passed over the left-hand thread.* When two pairs of adjacent threads are to be joined, this is done by crossing the two inside threads, *the thread on the left going over the thread on the right;* this process is called simply 'crossing'.

To summarise:

     turning: always right over left.

     crossing: always left over right.

A *pass* in bobbin lace making is a combination of crossing and turning. A pass is always made with two pairs, in other words with four threaded bobbins.

In fact, there are only two kinds of pass, and these form the whole foundation of lace making: they are known as the *gauze stitch* and the *cloth stitch*.

The gauze stitch consists of turning once and crossing once (this pass is discussed in greater detail on page 28).

19

The cloth stitch consists of crossing once, turning once, and crossing once (see Fig. 15, and page 21).

All other passes, which will be discussed later, are obtained by doubling one of these basic stitches, with or without the addition of further turnings.

For instance, a rose-net stitch consists of: a gauze stitch, pin, gauze stitch (see Fig. 16). This stitch is explained in detail on page 33.

A plait (Fig. 17) consists of three or more consecutive gauze net stitches, not pinned between each stitch. This pass is discussed in detail on page 29.

All that beautiful, intricate looking lace, both historical and modern, is based on the few passes mentioned above!

3. THE LANGUAGE OF SYMBOLS

The various movements in the lace patterns will be denoted by a number of rather algebraic looking symbols. This code was in fact adopted by the author to avoid long, repetitious lists of abbreviations, as in knitting patterns. Each pass or stitch in lace making is given its own symbol.

After working through some of the stitches, it will be seen that the symbols are not arbitrary, but that their shape reflects the passes they represent. A complete table of symbols, together with the movements they represent, will be found on page 70. The symbols are also printed on the back flap of the book jacket, for easy reference. The flap can simply be folded over any page that is being worked from.

Below is a list of the stitches and movements for which symbols are used in the patterns:

☐	Cloth stitch	××	Turning twice
⊡	Double cloth stitch	╳	Plait or braiding
△	Gauze stitch	✕	Passing with thick thread to the right
△	Rose-net stitch (double gauze stitch)	✕	Passing with thick thread to the left
•	Pin	≡	Point de reprise
×	Turning		
⇌	Direction in which the row is being worked (this will be followed by a symbol indicating the relevant stitch).		

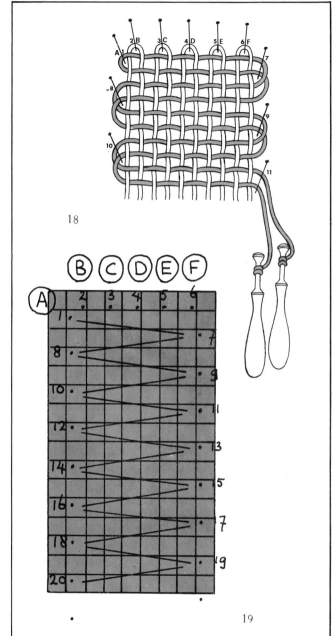

18

19

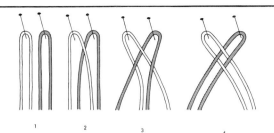

cloth stitch

INSTRUCTIONS IN SYMBOLS
FOR WORKING CLOTH STITCH

$(1) \leftarrow \square\ BCDEF \times\ .\ (7)$
$(8)\ .\ \times\ BCDEF\ \square \rightarrow A$
$A \leftarrow \square\ BCDEF \times\ .\ (9)$
$(10)\ .\ \times\ BCDEF \rightarrow\square\ A$
$A \leftarrow \square\ BCDEF \times\ .\ (11)$

and so on

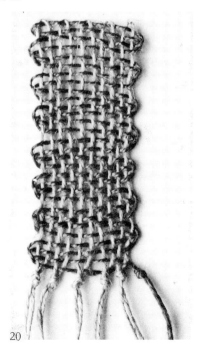

The cloth stitch is indicated by a small square, since, when completed, it resembles one. The double cloth stitch is the simple cloth stitch done twice, and pinned in between; this pin is the dot in the square. The gauze stitch, when completed, looks like a triangle, which is why this geometrical figure has been chosen to represent it. The double gauze stitch is: gauze stitch, pin, gauze stitch, with the pin represented as the dot in the triangle. Turning is quite obvious: the right-hand thread is crossed over the left-hand thread.

4. STARTING BOBBIN LACE MAKING

All the necessary equipment and materials for making bobbin lace have now been discussed, and a small experimental piece of lace, using the cloth stitch, should now be attempted.

A pattern, consisting entirely of cloth stitch, should be drawn up as shown in Fig. 19. This can either be done the same size as the actual work, or to scale on squared paper. With greater experience, it will be possible to work without the aid of a pattern, but the beginner certainly needs to use one.

A lace pattern is a drawing which indicates where the bobbins should start, and where the pins should be placed which will determine the ultimate shape of the work. The distance between the pins, together with the thickness of the yarn, will determine the degree of fineness of the lace.

Cloth stitch lace, when made correctly, has as many threads running crossways as lengthways. Depending on the kind of yarn being used, it may be found that the number of squares between the pins is either too large or too small. When one's first piece of lace has been made, it will be easier to judge the correct distances between the pins. These should be remembered for future use.

When trying out the first, sample pieces of lace, it is advisable to use smooth twisted yarn — 6/2 or 8/2 linen, for instance, or mercerised cotton (cotton which has been treated to make it smooth and shiny). Then the pattern in Fig. 19 can be followed exactly. If using a thinner type of yarn, such as real lace yarn, buttonhole silk, or fishing line, then the equivalent of one square in Fig. 19

should be taken as the distance between the pins, instead of one and a half squares.

The lace pattern, together with a piece of thin card, should be pinned to the pillow. It should be positioned a little above centre. This is easier to do if a thick book or similar object is put underneath the head of the pillow, so that it is tilted slightly towards one.

Now yarn of one colour should be wound on to five pairs of bobbins, and yarn of another colour on to a sixth pair.

The yarn is attached to the bobbin in the following manner. A length of yarn about 3 ft. 3 ins. (95 cm.) long should be doubled, and one end secured to the neck of the bobbin with a half-hitch (Fig. 21a, b, c). The bobbin is picked up in the left hand, and about half the length of of the yarn is wound on to the bobbin by turning it away from one (Fig. 21d). The yarn is finally secured with a loop (Fig. 21e). This loop enables the working thread to be lengthened without the knot having to be undone. The other end of the yarn is attached to a second bobbin with a half-hitch, and the other half of the complete thread is wound on to it. There is now a reserve of yarn on both bobbins, which should be linked together by an unwound length of yarn measuring about 4 ins. (10 cm.). A pin can now be stuck in at point 2 on the lace pattern (Fig. 19); about half the length of the pin, slanting backwards, should be pushed down into the pillow.

The linking thread between the bobbins is passed round the pin, and the bobbins are allowed to hang down. This pair will be known as pair B (see Fig. 19). The pin is pushed into the pillow slanting backwards because the bobbins will later have to be pulled downwards. The pins must always slant in the opposite direction to that in which the threads secured by them will be pulled.

Now yarn of the same colour should be wound on to four more pairs of bobbins. Pins should be stuck in at points 3, 4, 5, and 6; there should be a pair of bobbins hanging from each pin. Pair C hangs from point 3, pair D from point 4, pair E from point 5, and pair F from point 6.

Yarn of a different colour is wound on to another pair of bobbins (called pair A); this pair of bobbins will hang from the pin on point 1. Everything is now ready

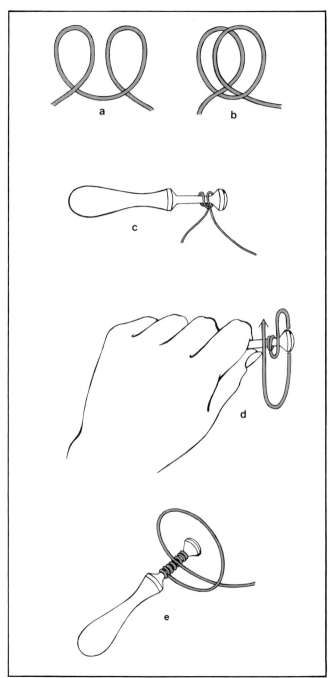

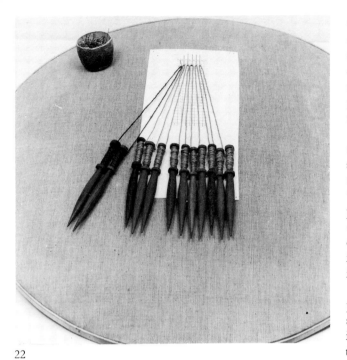

22

23

to start. The distances between all the pins and bobbins should be equal; this makes for much easier working, since the bobbins remain in place more easily. The use of a different coloured yarn on one pair of bobbins will make it easier to see what is happening as the lace pattern develops; it will also prevent confusion as to the exact position of the running pair.

This concept of a running pair of bobbins should be explained: in lace making, the bobbins are divided into active and passive pairs. The passive pairs, by definition, do very little work and are called 'hanging pairs' or 'passives'; the active bobbins are referred to as 'running pairs' or 'leaders'. All the movement in the pattern relies on the running bobbins, and they should have more yarn on them than the hanging pairs. This is worth bearing in mind when working on larger patterns, but it is less important with smaller, experimental pieces.

In this pattern, then, the running pair is pair A, and pairs B, C, D, E, and F are the hanging pairs. Simple step-by-step instructions follow. Exactly the same instructions, but in symbol language, will be found next to the photograph and drawing of cloth stitch lace (Fig. 20).

Pairs A and B are the pairs with which the first cloth stitch will be made. The right-hand thread of pair A is first crossed over the left-hand thread of pair B. Then the left-hand thread of pair A is turned over the left-hand thread of pair B, and the right-hand thread of pair B is turned over the right-hand thread of pair A. Now the right-hand thread of B is crossed by the left-hand thread of A. The first example of cloth stitch lace is now completed.

Pair B should be taken up in the middle with the thumb and index finger of the left hand, holding the index finger between the two bobbins. Pair A is taken in the right hand in exactly the same way; pair B is pulled obliquely towards the left, allowing the bobbins to rotate between the three fingers in which they are held. At the same time, pair A is pulled obliquely to the right, and allowed to rotate in a similar fashion (Fig. 23).

Rotating the bobbins allows the crossing of the threads to fall into place near the pin at point 2. This rotation should be done after every pass. With a little more experience, it can be done after each row has been completed; however this only applies to smooth yarn.

Pair B has now played its part; it should be put aside, and the bobbins secured with a pin. The cloth stitches are now continued with pairs A and C, then with pairs A and D, then A and E, and finally with A and F. This completes the first row.

A pin can now be inserted at point 7, and pair A turned once (in other words the right-hand thread is passed round the left-hand one). *Each time a row of cloth stitch lace is completed, one turn is made* (Fig. 24). If this is not done, the two threads of the running pair tend to lie untidily at the edge of the pattern. The bobbins are rotated once again to allow the new stitch to fall into place.

The cloth stitching is now repeated, using first pair A and pair F, then pair A and pair E, then A and D, A and C, and A and B, until point 8 is reached. Another pin is inserted there, the running pair is turned once, and from this point the patterns of the first and second rows are alternated. A very pretty piece of lace is now beginning to form.

If the same instructions are now read in symbol form, the symbols will begin to mean something. The direction of the arrows indicates whether the row is from right to left, or from left to right.

The lace can be left in place on the pillow, if desired, but the bobbins must first be secured on the pillow with ribbon and pins, or with string or elastic, which should be turned after each pin (Fig. 25). The pillow can now be picked up, and put away if necessary.

When enough cloth stitch lace has been made to give confidence in using the bobbins, the yarn can be cut about 4 ins. (9.6 cm.) from the end of the final row. The thread ends are then secured two by two with a knot. Now the pins can be removed, and a second sample begun. The bobbins should be tied up in twos, so that the pairs remain together. Further samples can be made using the same threads; it does not matter if they are knotted together.

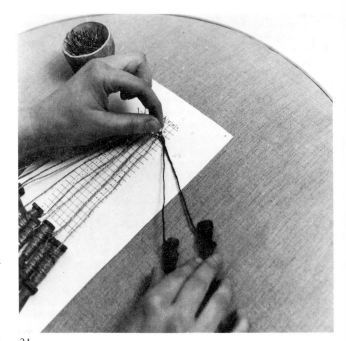

24

25

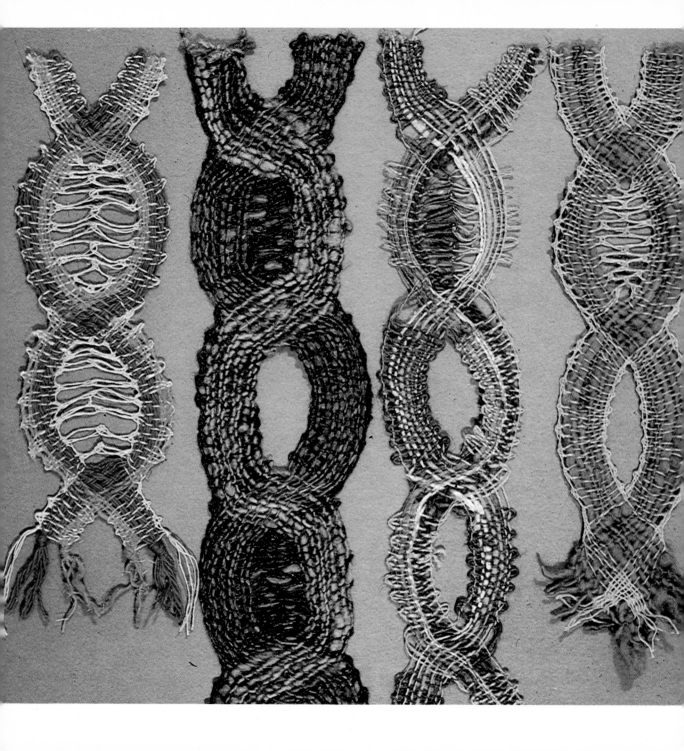

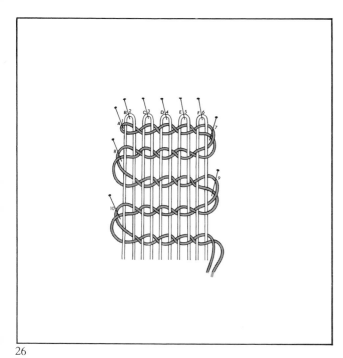

26

5. TURNING THE RUNNING PAIR FOR CLOTH STITCH

The same pattern can be used for the next sample, which is an exercise in cloth stitch, turning the running pair. Six pairs of bobbins will be needed: five pairs wound with 2 ply 6/2 yarn of one colour, and a sixth pair threaded with similar yarn, but in a contrasting colour.

In this sample, the running pair is turned once after passing each hanging pair (right-hand thread over left-hand thread). The hanging pairs must be well spaced out.

This particular way of working is especially suitable for free lace making if handspun wool is used for the hanging pairs. If thin yarn is used for the running pair, then the beautiful texture of the sheep's wool is shown to great advantage, since the thin yarn is hardly notice-able.

It may well be possible now to work directly from the symbols and the drawing (Fig. 26). It is advisable to cover everything with paper, except the row that is being worked at any one time.

Pair B is hung on point 2, pair C on point 3, D on 4, E on 5, and F on 6. These bobbins are all wound with thread of the same colour. Pair A is hung from point 1; the thread is again 6/2, but in a contrasting colour.

SYMBOLIC INSTRUCTIONS

$$A \rightarrow \square\,B \times C \times D \times E \times F \times \quad\bullet\quad (7)$$
$$(9)\ \bullet\ \times B \times C \times D \times E \times F\,\square \leftarrow A$$
$$A \rightarrow \square\,B \times C \times D \times E \times F \times \quad\bullet\quad (10)$$
$$(11)\ \bullet\ \times B \times C \times D \times E \times F\,\square \leftarrow A$$
$$A \rightarrow \square\,B \times C \times D \times E \times F \times \quad\bullet\quad (12)$$
$$(13)\ \bullet\ \times B \times C \times D \times E \times F\,\square \leftarrow A$$
$$A \rightarrow \square\,B \times C \times D \times E \times F \times \quad\bullet\quad (14)$$

and so on until the lace is the required length.

6. CLOTH STITCH AND ITS VARIATIONS

An attractive piece of lace can be made using cloth stitch only, with partial turning of the hanging pairs and the running pair.

Fig. 28 shows two lengths of lace, both made from the same pattern, but using very different materials. The

27

pattern had to be reduced for the much finer white lace, which would have been very loose and slack if the distance between the pins had been the same as for the coarser lace.

This sample of lace can be made longer if desired, but if so it is advisable to make the pattern at least 8 ins. (19.2 cm.) long, otherwise the lace will have to be pushed up every 2 ins. (4.8 cm.).

Six pairs of bobbins are needed. Four pairs are wound with handspun sheep's wool (dyed golden brown with heather, for instance); one pair with handspun sheep's wool (dyed green with sorrel); one pair (the running pair) with a coarse single ply thread.

The green pair B is hung on point 2. The brown pairs C, D, E, and F are hung on points 3, 4, 5, and 6. The running pair is hung on point 1. The hanging pairs E and F are turned after every row.

If the end of the pattern has been reached, and the work is intended to be a little longer, all the pins should be removed (without cutting the bobbins loose), and the finished work pushed upwards. The edge of the lace is then pinned down for about $\frac{3}{4}$ in. (18 mm.) to the top part of the pattern, and the pattern continued as before. The pins should be put back at each point where they were previously fixed.

28

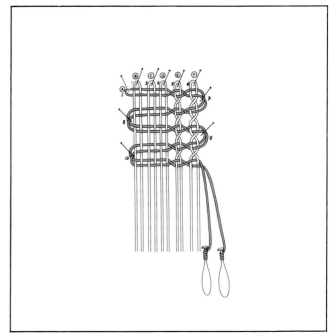

29

7. WHAT TO DO IF THE YARN BREAKS

This is what should be done when the end of the yarn is reached, or if it breaks.

About 2 ins. (4.8 cm.) of the broken yarn should be left hanging loose. A new thread of yarn is then wound on to the bobbin, and the end secured to a pin with a half-hitch; the pin is inserted in the section of lace already completed, about $\frac{1}{2}$ in. (12 mm.) above the point at which the work is being done (where the broken thread is hanging). When the lace is ready, the end of each thread is worked into the weave so that each overlaps by about $\frac{1}{2}$ or $\frac{3}{4}$ in. (between 12 and 18 mm).

The ends of both threads can also be knotted together in the following way: the right-hand thread is passed over the left one, making a knot, then the left is passed over the right, making another knot (Fig. 30).

SYMBOLIC INSTRUCTIONS

A → ☐ BCD × E × F × • (7)
         E ×   F ×
(8) • × BCD × E × F☐ ← A
         E ×   F ×
A → ☐ BCD × E × F × • (9)
         E ×   F ×
(10) • × BCD × E × F☐ ← A
         E ×   F ×
A → ☐ BCD × E × F × • (11)
         E ×   F ×
(12) • × BCD × E × F☐ ← A

and so on.

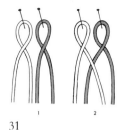

gauze stitch

31

8. EXAMPLE OF GAUZE STITCH

Gauze stitch is the other stitch on which bobbin lace making is based. As can be seen in Fig. 31, the second and fourth threads are turned across the first and third threads (right over left), and then both centre adjacent threads cross (left over right).

Six pairs of bobbins are needed: five pairs wound with the same colour of 6/2 yarn; and one pair with a yarn of similar texture but in a different colour. The pattern in Fig. 19 can be used.

Pairs B, C, D, E, and F are hung on points 2, 3, 4, 5, and 6 respectively; pair A, with its different coloured thread, is hung on point 1.

Pairs A and B are used in making the first gauze stitch; care should be taken that both pairs are always rotated properly. The left-hand pair is then put on one side, and another gauze stitch made with pair C. Again the left-hand pair is put to one side, and D is taken on the right. The gauze stitch is continued until point 7 is reached. A pin is inserted here, and, still using gauze stitch, point 8 is returned to. In this stitch, the bobbins in the running pair do not remain together. Only one thread from pair A is worked to and fro; the other is worked obliquely through the lace. The first A thread therefore takes up a new partner at every stitch. In the example (Figs. 32 and 33), this can easily be seen, since the thread of pair A is in a contrasting colour.

The logical development of gauze stitch is the plait. This is still essentially a gauze stitch, and the same two pairs of bobbins are used.

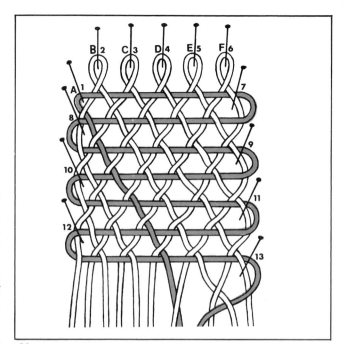

32

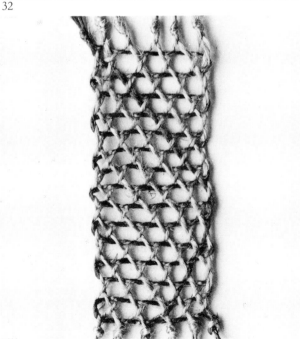

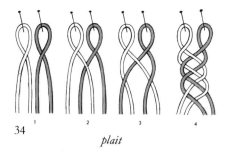

34

plait

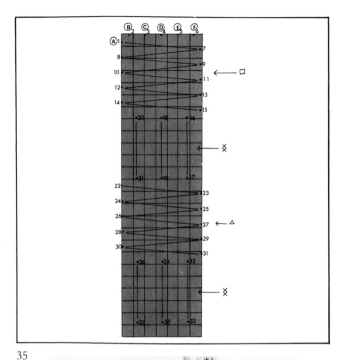

35

9. PLAITS MADE WITH TWO BOBBINS

There are quite a number of examples of lace from the beginning of the 16th century which consist entirely of plaits. These plaits were connected by cloth stitch at certain points to make larger pieces of lace. This kind of lace was not very different from the kind of braiding usually associated with the ends of weaves.

This lace was often made in red, blue, or yellow silk yarn. Gold and silver threads were sometimes used, too. The pieces of work were very strong and well-made, but very few have survived to the present day, since many of them were torn apart, in times of economic difficulty, for the gold and silver threads they contained.

A plait is made with two pairs of bobbins, in other words with four threads. The two pairs of bobbins can be hung from a pin in the pillow, and gauze stitches can then be executed one after the other, thus: turn and cross, turn and cross, as in Fig. 34. The symbol for a plait is two crosses, side by side.

In free lace, plaits can even be made with four pairs of bobbins, making the plait twice as thick.

10. LACE USING THREE STITCHES

This section is an exercise in making plaits as links between sections of gauze stitch lace and sections of cloth stitch lace. It will also serve as preparation for the lace curtain on page 38.

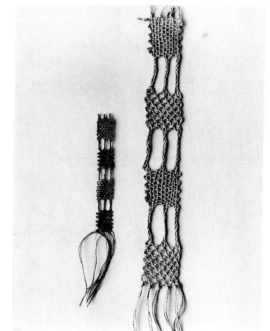

36

The lace shown in Fig. 36 can be done twice — once using 2 ply 6/2 yarn, and once with single ply 14/1 yarn (which is very thin). The size of the pattern in Fig. 35 is based on 6/2 yarn.

Six pairs of bobbins are needed, all wound with 2 ply 6/2 yarn of the same colour. Pairs A, B, C, D, E, and F are hung on points 1, 2, 3, 4, 5, and 6 respectively.

11. BLUE LACE

Modern lace making becomes much more interesting when yarn in a variety of colours and textures is used for cloth stitch and plaits, with additional turning.

Plate 4 shows two examples of lace made to exactly the same pattern. The only difference is that the light and dark colours and the thick and thin threads have been interchanged. This creates a completely different effect.

This piece of lace is made with eleven pairs of bobbins, following the pattern in Fig. 37. Turquoise, green, and blue-green yarn are used. Altogether, there are five thicknesses of yarn, distributed as follows: four pairs of threads in single ply turquoise smooth linen yarn; two pairs of threads in blue-green 14/1 linen yarn (one of these was used as the running pair in the lace in Plate 4 preceding page 41); two pairs of threads in blue-green coarse single ply 14/1 linen yarn; one pair of threads in green coarse single ply $2\frac{1}{2}$ yarn; and two pairs of threads in green coarse single ply 14/1 yarn.

This should only be taken as an example, since any harmonious blend of colours can be used, and no-one is likely to make exactly the same lace as the next person. It is an interesting exercise to see how the place of the hanging threads can be changed by using different stitches (cloth stitch in this case). The first part of this piece of lace is done entirely in cloth stitch, with two turns between pairs F and G, and two turns between J and K. In between the main sections of the piece of lace, pairs C and D go on point 21, E and F on 22, G and H on 23, I and J on 24, and K and L on 25, all connected by a row of cloth stitches. These pairs then turn once. Running pair A makes a plait with pair B from point 20 to point 26. Then the second section of the lace is made in the same way as the first. The mechanics of this can be seen in Fig. 38.

30

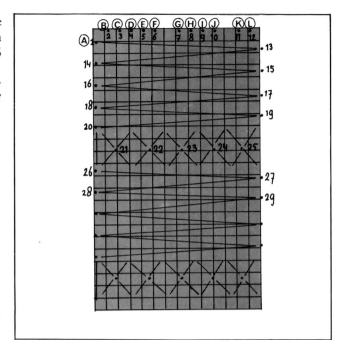

37

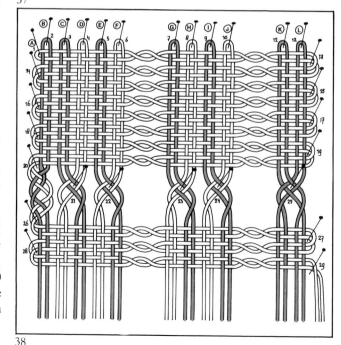

38

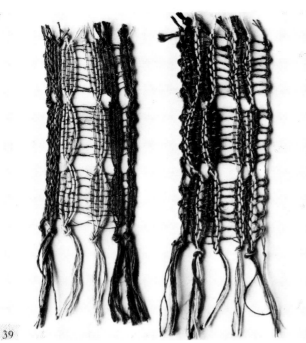

39

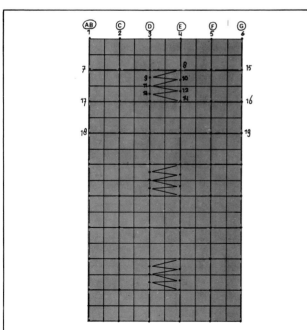

This example has been given to help readers to work out their own patterns. Even if no more than slight variations on these patterns can be achieved at first, this is a good beginning. Experimentation will produce ideas for new and original patterns.

12. POINT DE REPRISE

This piece of lace will give practice in doing cloth stitch with turns and plaits. At the same time it introduces a new kind of stitch known as point de reprise. This is a cloth stitch in which only one thread moves to and fro and up and down, instead of two threads as in the standard cloth stitch.

This stitch can be practised with two pairs of bobbins pinned up at two points on the pillow. The left thread of the right pair will 'run', while the right thread will 'hang' together with the threads of the left-hand pair (see Fig. 42).

It is a particularly useful stitch when making free lace, and strikingly different effects can be obtained by alternating smooth and rough yarn. Normally a very smooth surface will be created, but when making free lace, the stitch can be made as open or as closed as desired, since it will form a strong weave anyway.

For this exercise the following will be needed: six pairs of bobbins threaded with 6/2 linen yarn in one colour, and one pair with 6/2 linen yarn in a second colour. A pair of bobbins with the same colour yarn should be pinned to each of points 2, 3, 4, 5, and 6; two pairs with a different colour yarn are pinned to point 1.

Pairs C, D, E, F, and G are turned twice. A gauze stitch is made twice with pairs A and B (in other words, a plait); pairs A and B are crossed, and a pin inserted at point 7. The symbolic instructions on page 32 should then be followed. Thus the hanging pairs turn twice after every row of cloth stitches, but those used in the point de reprise or plaiting do not turn (see Figs. 39 and 42).

40

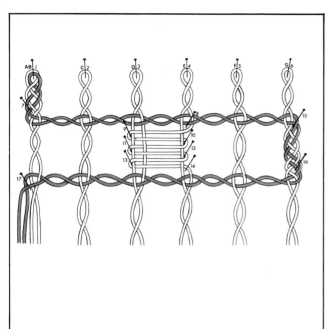

41

SYMBOLIC INSTRUCTIONS

A → □B2 × C2 ×D2 ×E2 ×F2 ×G : (15)

         D and E ≡ to point 14

        B2 × C2 ×F 2 ×A and G × (16)

(17) • × B2 × C2 ×D2 ×E2 ×F2 ×G□← A

A and B ×•(18)C2 ×D2 ×E2 ×F2 ×G2 ×

A → □B2 × C2 ×D2 ×E2 ×F2 ×G • (19)

and so on (see Fig. 40).

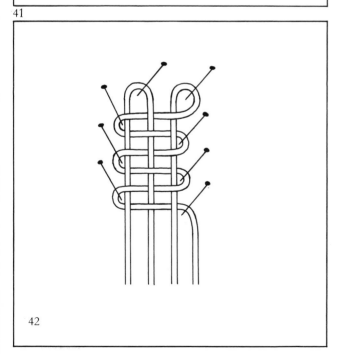

42

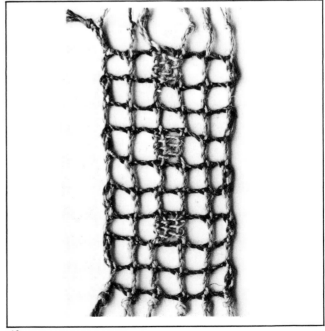

43

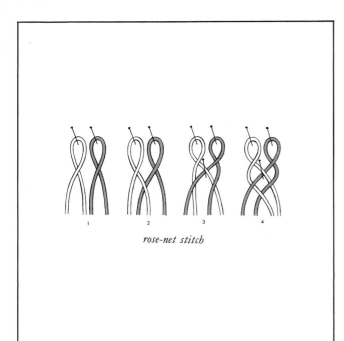

rose-net stitch

44

13. ROSE-NET STITCH

Rose-net is nothing more than a gauze stitch made with two pairs of bobbins, a pin between the second and third threads, and finally another gauze stitch with the two pairs of bobbins.

For the example illustrated here (Fig. 45), six pairs of bobbins are needed: four pairs with one colour, and two pairs with a contrasting colour. All the threads are 6/2 linen yarn.

Two pairs of bobbins with the same colour threads are pinned at points 1 and 3 in the pattern (Fig. 46). Two pairs with a contrasting colour are pinned at point 2.

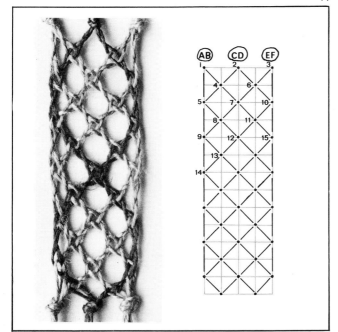

45

46

47

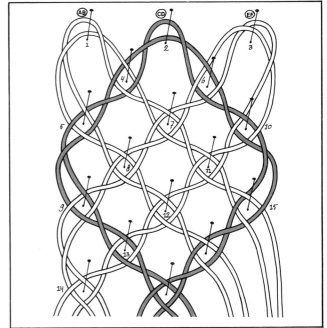

33

The pattern goes on like this:

to 4 △ BC	to 10 △ DF
to 5 △ AC	to 11 △ BF
to 6 △ DE	to 12 △ AF
to 7 △ BE	to 13 △ CF
to 8 △ AE	to 14 △ EF
to 9 △ CE	to 15 △ BD

and so on, for as long as required (see Fig. 47).

The work can be done in diagonal lines, in the order indicated by the numbers; or alternatively in vertical lines: first, 4 and 6, then 5, 7, and 10. It is faster, however, to work in diagonal lines, and clearer too.

If all these exercises are regularly practised, sufficient expertise will be acquired for decorative pieces of lace to be attempted, such as the one described in the next section.

14. GARLAND MADE WITH TWELVE PAIRS OF BOBBINS

This piece of lace consists entirely of cloth stitch and double cloth stitch, and is therefore suitable for beginners.

The term 'double cloth stitch' is a new one; it simply means a single cloth stitch, pin between second and third bobbins, then another cloth stitch. This stitch can be seen in the centre of the piece of lace in Fig. 48.

The materials used in this particular example were handspun sheep's wool and rough single ply linen yarn. The wool was coloured with the following plant dyes: elderberry (purple), red onions (golden yellow), and madder (red); the linen yarn was dyed in a blue-green cold water dye (see Plate 1 facing page 24). The sheep's wool was used for the hanging pairs, and the linen divided between the hanging and running pairs.

The required shape was cut out twice, as two curving but parallel lines. One was turned over and placed on top of the other to obtain the pattern required (Fig. 49). Next the pins were set up. The distance between the pins on the outside is slightly greater than between those on the inside.

Fig. 49 shows the actual pattern of the lace; Fig. 48 demonstrates the method. The final result can be seen in Fig. 50.

On each side of the layout for this piece of lace are the hanging pairs: three pairs of bobbins with sheep's wool, and two pairs with rough linen.

One pair of bobbins with sheep's wool is pinned to each of the points 2, 3, 4, and 8, 9, 10; one pair with tough linen yarn is pinned to points 1, 5, 7, and 11 respectively.

There are two running pairs — one pair for each leg of the lace. Rough linen yarn is used for both running pairs. Pair F should be pinned to point 6, and pair L to point 12.

Fig. 48 is drawn to the shape of the lace, and shows, stitch by stitch, exactly how this piece should be made. At first sight, it may look a little complicated; but it is in fact exactly the same until the middle of the piece is reached: two rows constantly repeated in both legs.

All the instructions have been written out completely to make them easier for the beginner. The same two rows are repeated until the narrower part of the pattern is reached, when all the pairs pass through each other. This is in fact half a raised plait — a technique which will be discussed later. After this, the same two rows are repeated again.

Only the first part of this lace is described here, because the rest is exactly the same, but in reverse.

To avoid confusion, it is best to start with the left-hand section, covering all the rows with paper except the one that is currently being worked on. If the arrow points towards the right (→), the row goes from left to right; if it points to the left (←), then the row goes in the opposite direction.

This particular example can also be made leaving the central part open. In this case, pairs F and L remain the running pairs throughout both sections of the work. The central part can also be made completely closed; in this case, while pairs F and L are used in exactly the same way, pairs A and K do the work of closing up the centre.

Plate 2 shows four examples of lace work done by different people after only five lessons.

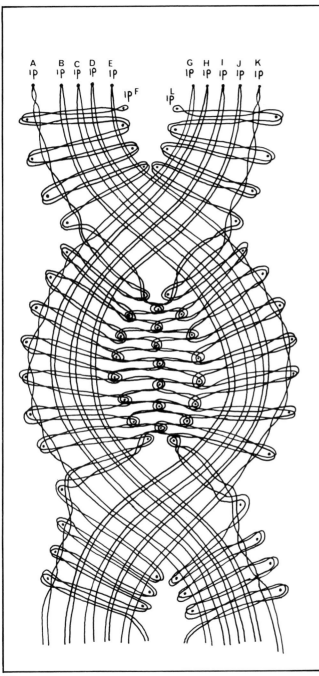

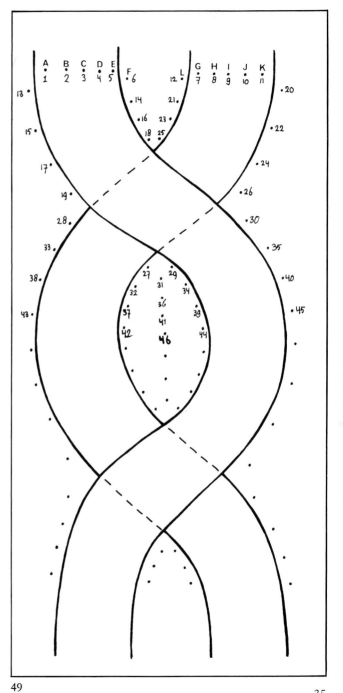

48

49

35

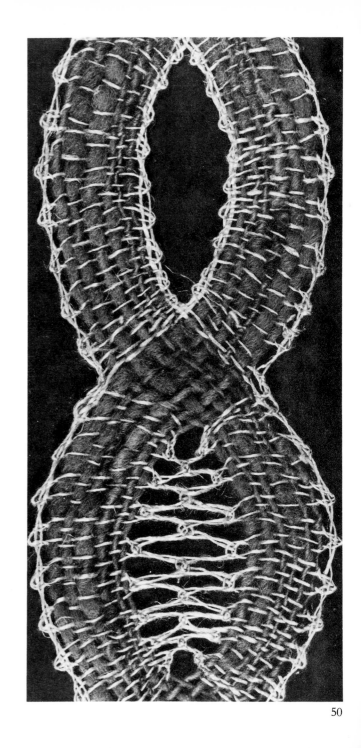

SYMBOLIC INSTRUCTIONS
← START HERE →

A ×
(13). ×A ×BCDE□ ← F
F → □A ×BCDE ×.(14)
A ×
(15). + A + BCDE□ ← F
F → □A ×BCDE ×.(16)
A ×
(17). ×A ×BCDE□ ← F
F → □A ×BCDE ×.(18)
A ×
(19) A □ ×BCDE□ ← F

×G BCDE□←G
    BCDE□←H
    BCDE□←I
    BCDE□←J

K ×
L → □GHIJ ×L ×.(20)
(21). ×GHIJ ×K□ ← L
K ×
L → □GHIJ ×L ×.(22)
(23). ×GHIJ ×K□ ← L
K ×
L → □GHIJ ×L ×.(24)
(25). ×GHIJ ×K□ ← L
K ×
L → □GHIJ ×□K (26)

A → □G ×HIJ ×
F → □G ×HIJ ×
       at 27□AF
A, F and G ×
(28). + G + HIJ□←A
A → □G ×HIJ ×
G ×

F   at 31 □ FL   L

×BCD ×E□ ← K
×BCD ×E□ ← L
    at 29□ I, K
K, L and F
K→□BCD ×E ×.(30)
×BCD ×E□ ← K
E ×

       at 32□AF
       A and F ×
(33). ×G ×HIJ□←A
A → □ ×HIJ
G ×

F   at 36□FL   L

    at 34□LK
    L and K ×
K→□BCD ×E ×.(35)
BCD ×E□ ← K
E ×

       at 37□AF
       A and F ×
(38). ×G ×HIJ□←A
A → □G ×HIJ ×
G ×

F   at 41□FL   L

    at 39□LK
    L and K ×
K→□BCD ×E ×.(40)
×BCD ×E□ ← K
E ×

       at 42□AF
       A and F ×
(43). ×G ×HIJ□←A
A → □G ×HIJ ×
G ×

       at 46□FL

From this point on,
work the pattern
F ×   in reverse   ×L

    at 44□LK
    L and K ×
K→□BCD ×E ×.(45)
×BCD ×E□ ← K
E ×

15. SMALL CURTAIN MADE IN CLOTH STITCH, GAUZE STITCH, ROSE-NET, AND PLAITS

This, is certainly a more ambitious piece of lace making for the comparative beginner. The dimensions are 3 ft. 9 ins. ×1 ft. 3 ins. (108 cm. ×36 cm.). This curtain was not in fact made on a pillow, but on a sheet of cork covered with paper (see Fig. 4). The pattern was drawn on the paper. When the curtain in Fig. 51 was made, the cork was held lengthways, but it is fact easier to use it diagonally, drawing the pattern accordingly. There will then be more room for laying the bobbins down; if the cork is used lengthways, they tend to fall off at the sides.

The measurements of each little block of close lace are $3\frac{1}{5}$ ins. $\times$ $3\frac{1}{5}$ ins. (8 cm. $\times$ 8 cm.). There are twelve such blocks in each strip; the strips are made up as in Fig. 52. In block 4 of the left-hand strip the symbols ☐‖☐ appear. This means that two blocks, each measuring $3\frac{1}{5}$ ins. $\times$ $1\frac{1}{5}$ ins. (8 cm.) $\times$ 4 cm), are worked in cloth stitch. There are also blocks in which the pairs of bobbins become divided into three groups. The centre part continues to be worked in cloth stitch, while the two sides develop into plaits. There is a plait beneath block 3 in the left-hand strip which passes to the middle strip to help work the fourth block in that strip. Each time such a plait appears in the diagram it means that one pair of bobbins has been passed over from one strip to another to continue working there. This pair of bobbins will return to its original strip after one or more blocks.

To make the curtain, twenty-four pairs of bobbins are needed. A very thick rough linen thread (3/2) was used for the curtain in Fig. 51. Eight pairs of bobbins are pinned above each of the three strips-to-be. All pairs should be turned two or three times, so that a metal or wooden rod can be attached later. The left-hand strip is worked up to and including the third block. Then one pair of bobbins is passed over to the centre strip, the first block of which is now worked. After this first block, one pair of bobbins is moved over to the right. Two more blocks, then the fourth block, of the middle strip are completed; at this point the pair of bobbins which has come from the left-hand strip can be taken up and worked with as well. Five blocks of the left-hand and

38

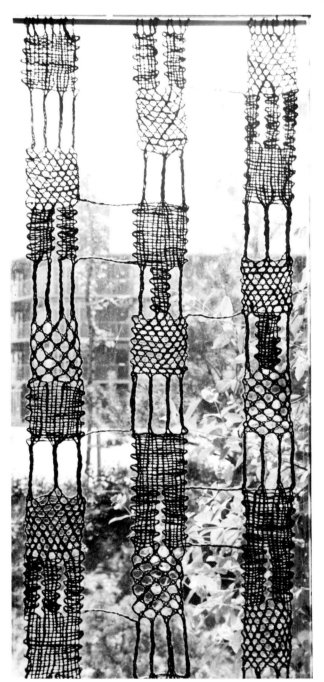

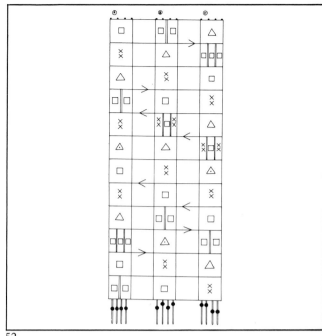

52

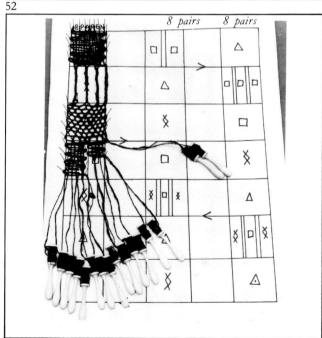

8 pairs   8 pairs

53

middle strips can now be completed. One pair of bobbins will come over from the right-hand to the middle. This means that the right-hand strip must be worked before going any further. After that, the instructions can be followed straight through. The beginning of the first strip can be seen in Fig. 53; in Fig. 54, the other strips have been added.

The particular curtain shown in the illustrations was continued until there was no more space in which to place the bobbins easily. Then all the pins were removed, and the curtain was moved upwards. Fig. 55 shows how the work was continued. The last blocks to have been completed were secured at the top of the cork with pins. Fig. 56 shows the curtain almost finished; when twelve blocks had been completed for each strip, the bobbins were cut away, leaving about 8 ins. (20 cm.) of loose yarn beneath. These threads were then knotted, and beads added to them for greater decorative effect. The pins were only removed when all the threads had been cut to the same length. The curtain was now ready for hanging; for this an aluminium strip was used, about $\frac{1}{5}$ in. wide, 16 ins. long and $\frac{1}{8}$ in. thick ($5 \times 384 \times 3$ mm.), but obviously a thin wooden rod, or any other suitable rod, can be used instead.

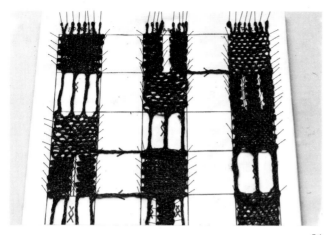

54

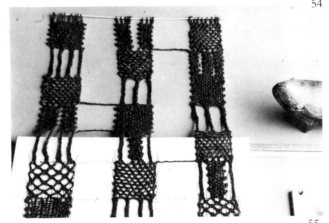

55

56

16. A THREE-DIMENSIONAL PROJECT

Here is a technique which is very useful to ·know, especially when making free bobbin lace, since it is both simple and versatile. The background of any piece of lace in which an outlining thread is used must obviously be quite thin, otherwise the lines traced by the thread will not stand out clearly. A rose-net background is very suitable for this kind of work; it also has the advantage of making it difficult for the thread to slip.

This section provides two examples, with instructions and a diagram, of how to pass a thread through a background. This type of lace looks very attractive in white or cream. Fig. 63 and Plate 4 preceding page 41 show the results of passing a thick thread through a background in graceful curves.

After the last stitch of the rose-net is made, the threads are turned twice before the thicker thread begins to be passed through. This can be seen in Fig. 57A; the bobbins must be imagined lying under each pair of threads. In Fig. 57B, the thick thread makes its first move to the right — in other words it takes up a position between the two threads of a pair. In Fig. 57C, the right-hand thread (the white one here) has been passed over the thick thread and right over its own partner thread; the two threads have thus already turned once. Fig. 57D shows the final phase: the pair of white threads is turned once more; this turn is in fact the beginning of the next gauze stitch.

Fig. 58 shows what happens when the thread is on the other side. Whenever a pair is to turn, it is always from right to left. In Fig. 58A, the gauze stitch has been completed, and both white threads are turned twice. Fig. 58B shows how the thick thread has been moved towards the left. Fig. 57C shows the left-hand white thread lying across the thick thread; however this left-hand white thread cannot go over the right-hand white thread, since this would involve a turn from right to left, which is not allowed; it must therefore go to the left of the right-hand thread. Finally, Fig. 58D shows the right-hand white thread turned once over the left-hand one, and, in Fig. 58E, twice. Here too, this turn is the beginning of the next gauze stitch, which completes the process.

Example I. Eleven pairs of bobbins are needed, wound

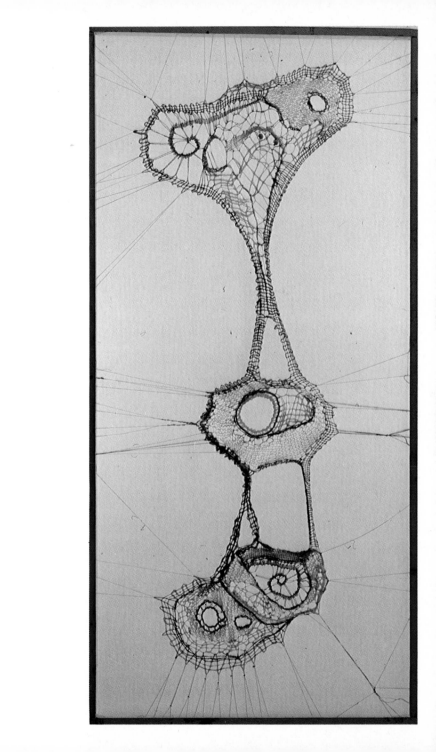

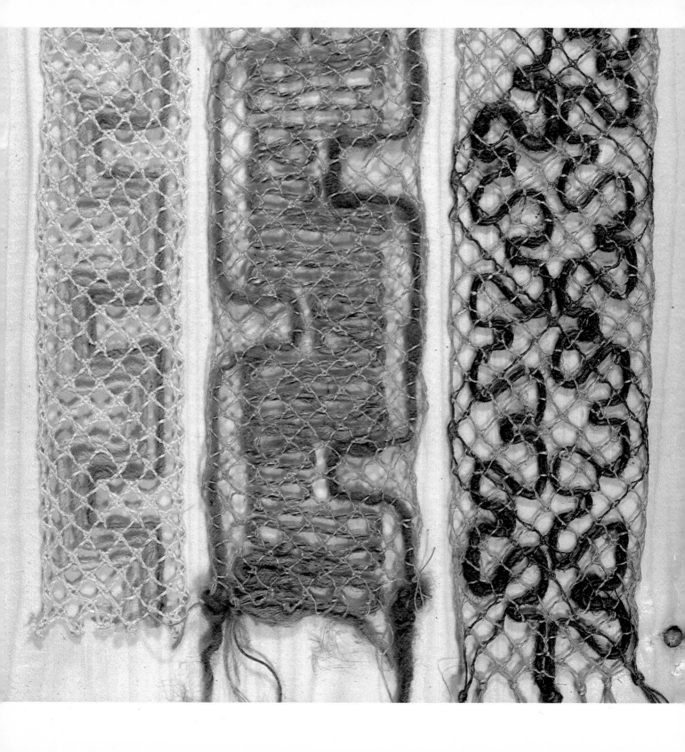

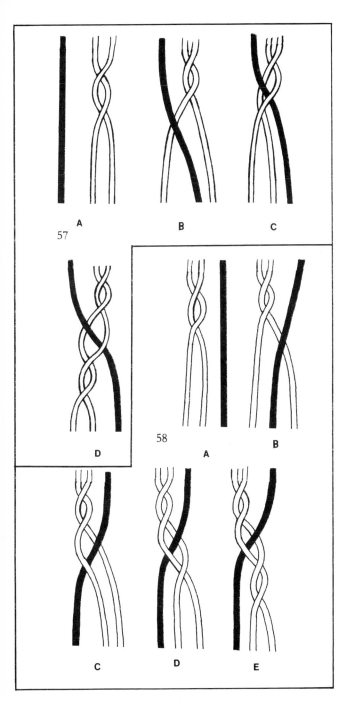

A

57

B

C

D

58

A

B

C

D

E

with a thin, rough, single ply or 2 ply linen yarn; and three thicker, coloured threads which are each wound on a single bobbin (in the lace illustrated in Fig. 63, cow-hair is used for the thick thread).

The pattern for this example is given in Fig. 59. The whole pattern should be copied on to graph paper, so that the direction in which the thicker threads are to be passed, immediately beneath the work, can be seen.

In Fig. 61, the pin points have been indicated where the pairs of bobbins meet. This has been done to avoid needless complication, since the pairs sometimes change places. The pairs are designated according to the code of the point they have just passed, though occasionally a right-hand or left-hand pair moving from a particular point is mentioned, where it has been impossible to do otherwise. A pair is designated by the letters of the point it has just left and the point it is going to, since this connection has to be indicated.

Two pairs of bobbins with the rough linen yarn are pinned to each of points A, B, C, D, and E; one pair only is pinned to point F (this pair will be needed to make the right-hand edge; if two pairs were pinned up, then there would be one over). Two of the three bobbins wound with thick thread are hung one on each side of point B, but slightly higher. The third one is hung to the left of point C.

If the lace is examined closely, it will be seen that there is one row through which the thick thread is passed, followed by one row of rose-net, and so on. When the thick thread has been passed through a pair of the basic threads, they are turned twice; this is also the beginning of the next rose-net stitch.

All the hanging pairs ×

row 1: thread 1 ✕ pair BG; thread 2 ✕ BH; thread 3 ✕CH;

row 2: △ to G from AB; △ to H from BC; △ to I from CD; △ to J from DE and △ to K from EF; all pairs ×. The left-hand pair from A and the right-hand pair from K ✕✕ to bridge the gap to the following point gracefully. The pairs GM, HM, and HN × an additional time, since the thicker thread has to pass through them.

row 3: thread 1 ✕ pair GM; thread 2 ✕ pair HM; thread 3 ✕ pair HN.

row 4: △ to L from AG; △ to M from GH; △ to N from HI; △ to O from IJ; △ to P from JK; all pairs × (left-hand pair from L × ×). Where a thick thread passes all pairs, turn an additional time before this thread makes its first pass.

row 5: thread 1 ✕ pair MQ; thread 2 ✕ pair MR; thread 3 ✕ pair RN, × pair NS, × pair OS, × pair OT, and × pair PT.

row 6: △ to Q from LM; △ to R from MN; △ to S from NO; △ to T from OP; △ to U from PK; all pairs × (right-hand pair from U × ×).

row 7: thread 1 × pair GW, × pair RW, × pair RX, × pair SX, × pair SY; × pair TY; thread 3 × pair TZ.

row 8: △ to V from LQ; △ to W from QR; △ to X from RS; △ to Y from ST; △ to Z from TU; all pairs × (right-hand pair from U × ×).

It should now be possible to continue without further instructions, if Fig. 61 is kept well in mind, and a row of passing the thread is alternated with a row of rose-net.

Example II. To make this lace (Fig. 63), fourteen pairs of bobbins are needed, wound with a thin, rough, single ply or 2 ply linen yarn, and one pair of bobbins with thicker yarn (2 ply linen yarn, for instance, if single ply is used on the other bobbins).

The pattern for this piece of lace is shown in Fig. 60, and can be copied on to graph paper. The working method is shown in Fig. 62. Two pairs of bobbins with the rough linen yarn are pinned to each of the points A, B, C, D, E, and F. The pair with the thicker thread is pinned above point D. (Since there are not enough letters in the alphabet to denote all the points, lower-case letters will be used after Z.)

As in the first example, whenever a thick thread is passed between two others, those threads turn an extra time before the work is continued.

All pairs ×, except the pair with the thick thread.

row 1: left-hand section of thick thread ✕ DJ; right-hand section of thick thread ✕ DK.

row 2: △ to H from AB ×; △ to I from BC; △ to L from EF; △ to M from FG ×; all pairs × (left-hand pair from A and right-hand pair from G × ×).

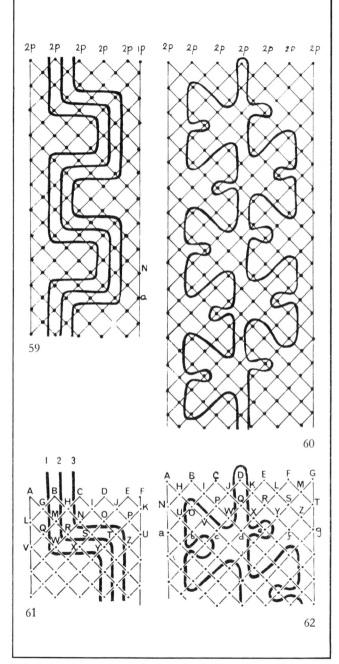

59

60

61

62

42

row 3: left-hand thread ✕ → JQ; right-hand thread ✕ → KQ; △ to Q from JK ✕; left-hand thread ✕ → QW; right-hand thread ✕ → QX.

row 4: △ to N from Ah ✕; (left-hand pair from H ✕ ✕); △ to P from 1J ✕; △ to W from PQ ✕; △ to R from KL ✕; △ to S from LM ✕; △ to T from MG ✕ (right-hand pair from T ✕ ✕); △ to X from QR ✕; △ to Y from RS ✕; △ to Z from ST ✕.

row 5: left-hand thread ✕ → Wc; ✕ → PV; ✕ → IO; HO.

row 6: △ to IO from HI ✕; left-hand thread ✕ → OU; △ to U from NO ✕; △ to a from NU ✕; △ to V from OP ✕; left-hand thread ✕ → Ub; △ to b from UV ✕; right-hand thread ✕ → Xd; ✕ → Xe; ✕ → Ye; △ to e from XY ✕; △ to f from YZ ✕; △ to g from ZT ✕.

row 7: △ to c from YZ ✕; △ to d from WX ✕.

It should now be possible to continue without further instructions, closely following Figs. 60 and 62.

17. MAKING A SMALL RAISED PLAIT

An insertion, or raised plait, is something which is seen frequently in old lace, and Figs. 66 and 67 show exactly how it is done.

Six pairs pass through each other, using a cloth stitch, after turning once. A pin is then inserted between the third and fourth pairs. Then all pairs resume their place, turn once, and then continue. The plait can be made with either one or two pins, but this makes no difference at all to the method used.

This technique should now be attempted in a piece of lace (Fig. 64) in which the plait will be surrounded by a rose-net background. This pattern is made with twelve pairs of bobbins, all wound with 2 ply 6/2 linen thread of the same colour.

Two pairs of bobbins are pinned to points 2, 3, 4, 5, and 6 respectively (see Fig. 65). One pair each is pinned to points 1 and 7. These pairs are used to make the rose-net, beginning with A and B at point 8. The numbers should be followed until point 36, when a pair of bobbins is pinned to each of points 19, 20, 21 and 32, 33, 34. The pairs of bobbins pinned to these points are the ones mentioned above; after turning twice, these

63

64

pairs pass through one another, as shown in Figs. 66 and 67. The central pin is inserted at point 37. All six pairs which are being used to make the insertion then turn once.

The rose-net recommences at point 38, and continues until point 71. This lance can be made to any length, simply by repeating the numbered diagram.

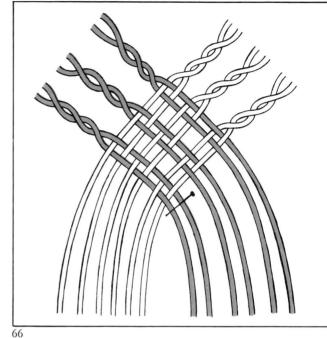

65

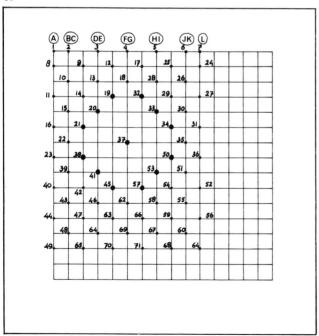

44

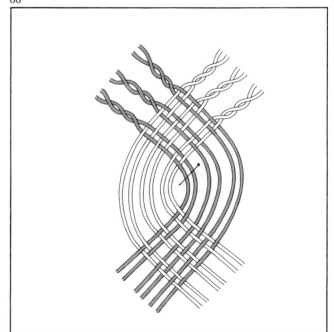

66

67

Creative lace making

1. HOW TO BEGIN CREATIVE LACE MAKING

Now that the basic principles of bobbin lace making have been mastered, it will be possible to make and adapt some of the exciting laces illustrated on the next few pages.

Ready-drawn patterns cannot be provided. Indeed, the whole excitement of creative bobbin lace making lies in the fact that the result will always be a completely individual, unique work, possibly inspired by some object which is interesting in colour or texture or both.

Here are a few examples of the kind of thing which may give inspiration to the creative lace maker: shells, fungi, moss, aerial photographs of volcanic craters and landscapes, photographs of human or animal tissues under the microscope, horse chestnut shells, tree bark, cut sections of fruit and vegetables, or raindrops running down a window pane. This is just an arbitrary list, and many more suitable subjects will be noticed by looking carefully in the home or in the countryside.

The chosen subject is copied on to a piece of paper. No special talent for drawing is needed, since the subject is merely copied as if it were a flat surface.

If the work is to consist of several pieces, the drawing must be cut up into several parts; a pattern is then made for each of these individual parts. Afterwards, all the parts can be joined together again, using the loose thread ends, to form a single piece of work.

The cutting-up solution presents several advantages: it is easier to handle smaller pieces, and fewer bobbins are needed. There is also the possibility of making the work even more interesting, since the linking of the separate parts can form an important feature of the overall design.

There are several ways of linking the parts: sewing the parts together by needle-stitching the end threads, such as in the 'Embryo' and 'Moss' designs described a little later on; knitting them together (see Fig. 103); or crocheting. Controlled use of macramé knots can also give exciting results.

It must be decided in advance exactly where to begin and where to end. The component parts must also be planned in such a way that the end threads do not finish up all bunched together — (it will be clear by now that the number of end threads on a piece of bobbin lace can be large). The more dispersed they are over the various parts of the design, the easier it will be, when joining up the individual parts, to use the end threads as an integral part of the whole design.

To provide a little assistance to start the reader off, the working method for the 'Thorn apple' design has been described very carefully, and there is even a photograph of the fruit used for the original design.

A drawing of the fruit, magnified five times, was made on white cartridge paper. A black felt pen was used, so that the lines would be easily visible when working. The paper, with the design on it, was pinned to the pillow. Then a method of working had to be evolved so that all the end threads would be left at the top (this seemed logical enough, since this was where the stalk joined the fruit).

Next, the best materials to use had to be considered. The inside work was to have strong contour lines, and therefore thick yarn was chosen for this. Thin linen yarn was used for the delicate lines at the point of the fruit.

It was not decided in advance what kind of stitch to use; this was to be dictated exclusively by the lines in the design. While working, it had to be decided where the lace was to be tight, and where it was to be loose. Plate 6 preceding page 49 shows how different people interpreted this design according to their different abilities and personalities.

A piece of lace which is to be divided into different parts can be begun like this. Examine carefully the two halves of a pepper, an onion, a red cabbage, and an apple. Then the outlines of these vegetables should be drawn and filled in a little. They do not have to be absolutely exact.

These drawings are then cut out and laid on another piece of paper, to form a pleasing composition. The drawings should not be placed too close to each other: 1 in. (24 mm.) apart is ideal. The outlines of the drawings can then be traced round as they lie on the paper.

The materials must now be selected. It is not advisable to use too many colours; a finer effect can be achieved by using two or three different shades of the same colour, or else different yarns, such as handspun wool, thin linen, cotton, or sewing silk in more or less the same colour. The drawing of one of the subjects can now be pinned up on the pillow together with a larger, thicker piece of drawing paper.

If a particular line needs to be very heavy and marked, then obviously thick yarn should be used. Thin yarn is more suitable for the delicate parts, to give a transparent effect. The end threads must come out at an appropriate place.

Each finished lace vegetable can be put down on the original draft, to see what has happened to the original composition. If this no longer seems right, the position of the parts can be moved round until the arrangement is satisfactory.

All the finished parts are pinned down on the pillow in the chosen arrangement. Then they must be linked up with a lace needle, taking care not to disturb the contours of the composition, and making sure that the actual joining does not dominate the main design. A sensible solution is to join similar colours in the different parts by means of the end threads. It is very important that colours should not come to an abrupt end anywhere; this would make them stand out too conspicuously in the overall design. Bold and exciting lines should be maintained throughout the work.

2. SUITABLE SUBJECTS

Here are some photographs which might well provide inspiration for creative lace making; many of these can be found in one's own environment, and studied at first-hand.

Fig. 68: Even vegetables can be exciting, if the right ones are chosen.

Fig. 69: Photograph of jawbone tissue under the microscope, magnified many times. (Photograph by courtesy of the Institute of Dentistry, University of Zürich.)

Fig. 70: Encrusted mussel shell.

Fig. 71: Section of a reed, seen under the miscroscope.

Fig. 72: Piece of moss (see page 57).

68

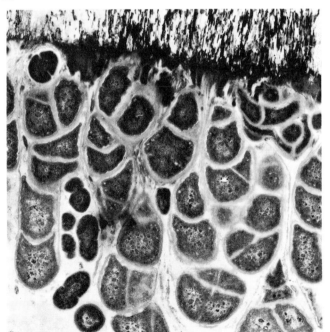

69

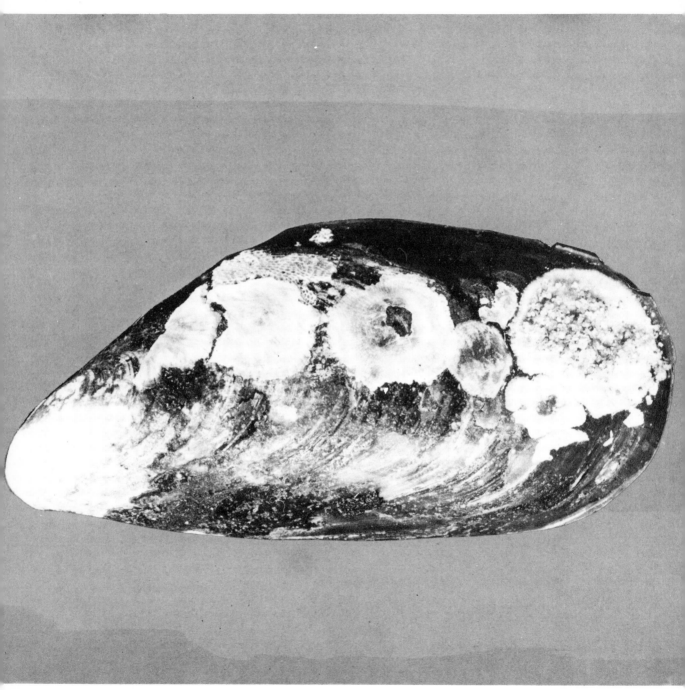

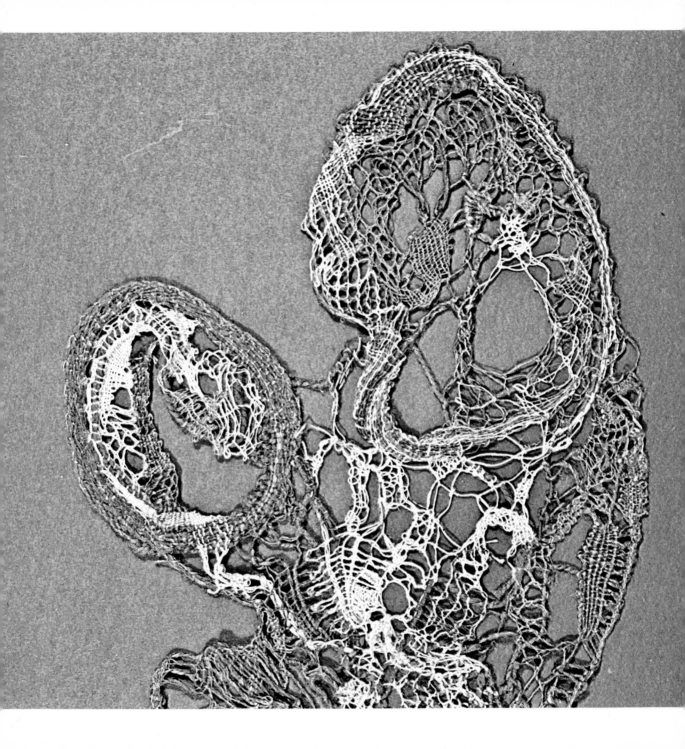

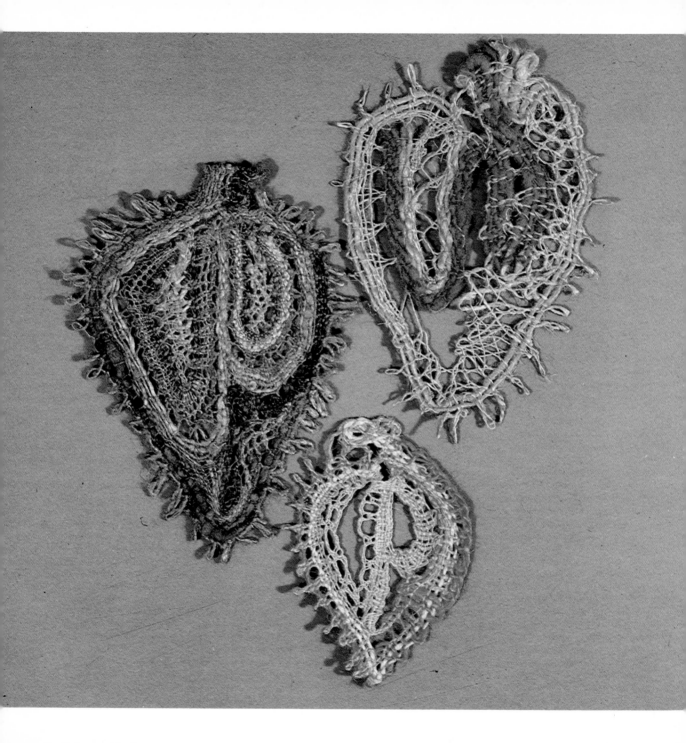

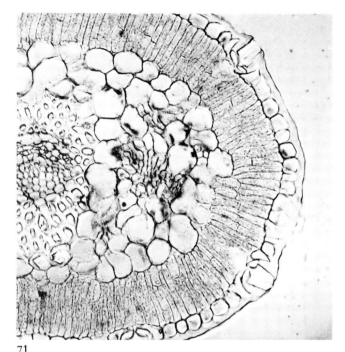

71

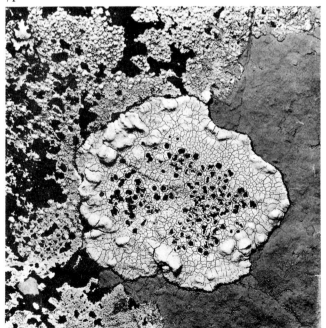

72

3. THORN APPLE

This is the first exercise in working without a strict pattern, and without regard for straight lines.

The original thorn apple (Fig. 73) used in this design came from a tree in the author's own garden. When opened, a network of fine lines is revealed — an ideal subject for a piece of free bobbin lace. The first step is to draw the thorn apple (Fig. 74), accentuating the lines of the membranes and the outline.

For starting the round contours in the centre, hand-spun wool is suitable, used principally on the hanging pairs. One pair of bobbins is pinned to points A and B (see Fig. 75). Another pair is then wound with thick, rough, handspun linen yarn, and pinned to point C; two pairs wound with thin, rough linen yarn are pinned to points D and E. A pair of bobbins wound with rough linen yarn of average thickness is also pinned to point C, to become the running pair (see Fig. 75). This pair is worked downwards in cloth stitch, passing to and fro through pairs A, B, C, D, and E. When the curve is reached, the pillow should be turned round and the curve completed in cloth stitch. When the curve is completed, the running pair is worked into the finished cloth stitch section on the other side. When the running pair reaches the inside of the curve, it should turn once or more, the number of times depending on the distance which has to be bridged. A pin head or thin crochet hook is then inserted through the turning loop of the running pair in the section already finished. Through this loop, one thread of the running pair is picked up. The other bobbin of the running pair is then slipped through this loop, rounded end first. The first bobbin can now be tightened to hold the stitch firm. All these movements are shown in Figs. 77 and 78.

The running pair now turns again once or more, and then the cloth stitch is continued through the thick pair in which the inner part of the thorn apple is outlined. Once the outer edge of this section has been reached in cloth stitch, the running pair turns, is pinned, and then moves back towards the middle section. It is then possible to turn back and make an attachment with a loop on the other side; the attachment can be made to both threads of the turning loop, or to one only, creating a lighter effect.

This can be continued until point F is reached, where the hanging pairs are divided into two groups. The thick and thin linen threads will form the outer contour line on the left, while the inside contour on the right will be formed by the handspun wool. Either the outer part on the left, or the inner part on the right, can be done first.

If the outer part is chosen, a new technique will have to be used. A way to create the effect of spikes on the thorn apple must be found. Fig. 81 shows how this can be done, using loops or picot stitches. After the linen thread has been cloth stitched through the hanging pairs towards the outside, the running pair turns once, and a pin is inserted between the two threads, before these are turned once more. Then the thread is cloth stitched back through the hanging pairs towards the inside of the thorn apple. The running pair turns once or twice, and is then attached to a turning loop made by the running pair at the start of the cloth stitch section. The outer contour is returned to, working through it in cloth stitch, and making loops if desired.

A longer tail can be made in this way by turning the running pairs twice or more before inserting a pin between the threads, and then turning back again.

The work is continued in this fashion until the point of the fruit is reached. Here, the thin linen threads come together with the running pair to form a rose-net pattern (gauze stitch, pin, gauze stitch). One pair is passed from time to time through the thick threads, both to hold them in place and to form the picots. A wider area of cloth stitch at the pointed end reproduces the membranes of the fruit. Once more the outlining threads are secured at the beginning.

When this point is reached, the right-hand inside contour must be made in cloth stitch with handspun wool and a pair of thin linen threads, in the same way as the left-hand inside section. Do not forget the attachment to a loop in the section which is already finished. The linen threads used in the outer left-hand section can then be worked up into the thicker inner part, and finished off in the outer right-hand section, moving upwards until the top is reached (point G), where all the threads come out together.

Plate 6 preceding page 49 shows the author's own lace

73

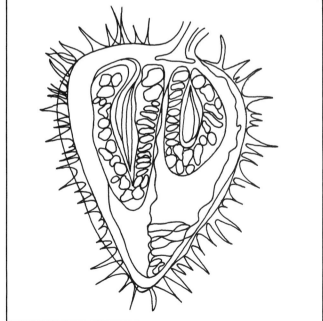

74

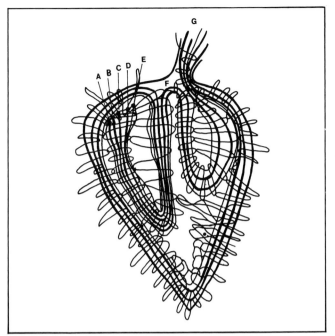

75

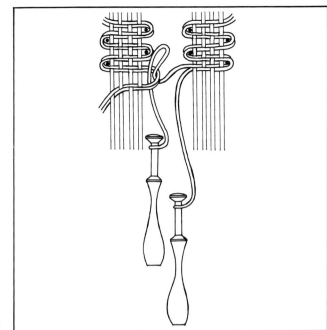

77

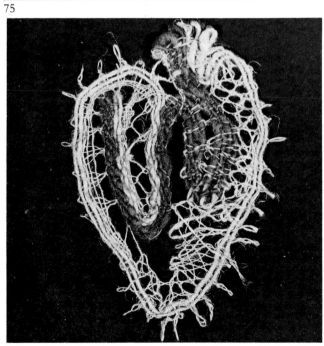

76

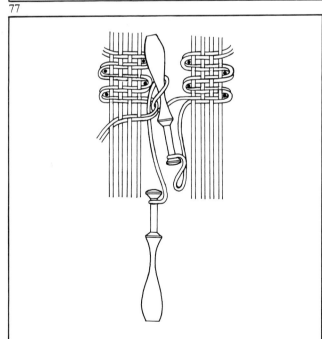

78

thorn apple, followed by two other thorn apples, worked by different people, but using the same pattern. They followed exactly the same diagram, starting in the same place, yet the final result is completely different, as can be seen. This is the beauty of creative lace making.

A good plan for a larger work on the same theme would be to draw the fruit and flowers of the same plant, and then work these separately. If using the same kind of yarn and similar colours, these separate parts can then be sewn together with a lace needle, using the end threads. The 'Embryo' design, which follows, describes how to make needle lace.

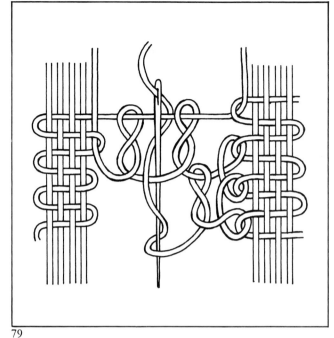

79

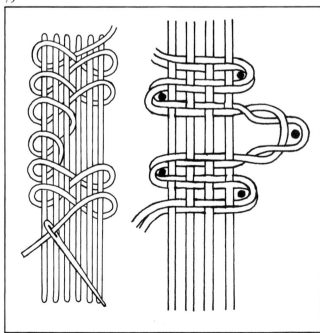

80   81

82

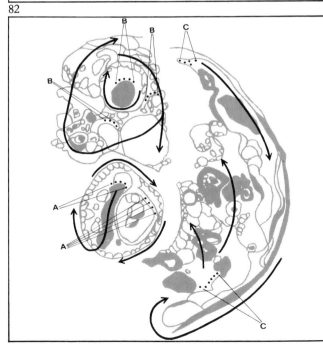

83

4. EMBRYO

'Embryo' seemed a suitable name for this design, though the actual inspiration was in fact a photograph of a tiny single-cell organism under the microscope.

When the design was copied, both the outline and the lines insides were enlarged. Then the subject was divided into four parts, since, as already mentioned, free bobbin lace making often produces more exciting results if each piece is made in separate parts which are then sewn together with needle lace stitches.

The work is begun at the rounded section A (see Fig. 83); a number of bobbins wound with linen thread are pinned to the points marked A in the centre. The work is continued in the direction of the arrow, taking care not to use thick yarn on the running pair, which would unbalance the pattern by making this particular thread stand out too much.

Then more bobbins are attached to points A, by looping them to the turning loops already there (see Figs. 77 and 78), or by pinning them to a suitable place and allowing them to function as hanging or running pairs.

After the completion of section A, the lace is re-started at the points marked C in the upper part of section C. When the curved part of C is complete (see curved arrow) new threads are needed to complete the wider part. These are therefore pinned to the points marked C at the foot of this section. The end threads are not cut off or worked in again, but simply left to hang.

Section B is also made up following Fig. 83. The work is begun at the points marked B on the central dark section, and then continued in the direction indicated by the arrow. Then new bobbins are hung on the points marked B to the right of the centre. When the points marked B beneath the centre and to the left are reached, the process has to be repeated again.

The importance of working a thick thread through the pattern to emphasise the various constituent forms of the design can be seen to great advantage in section B. The next task, of course, is to dispose of all the hanging threads.

Sections A, B, and C are first pinned to the pillow, about 2 ins. (4.8 cm.) being left between each section.

As far as possible, similarly coloured threads, and threads from different sections, are placed together; for instance, one colour area in section A was matched in this example with a similar colour area in section B. It is very important to avoid bringing the development of any colour or shade to an abrupt halt.

Then the end threads are sewn together or worked back into their own sections, as appropriate, using a kind of slip stitch similar to a blanket stitch, with some variations like looping the thread over the needle.

To practise these stitches, it is a good idea to start by cutting out a rectangle of thin card measuring about 2 ins. $\times$ $3\frac{1}{5}$ ins. (4.8 cm. $\times$ 7.6 cm.). Start at point A and go straight to B, where the needle is turned round the card, and then return, making loops all along AB, as shown in Fig. 84. This process is repeated to C, then D and E, making loops through the other loops. This simple technique will be mastered quickly.

Fig. 85 shows how to link up a thread from the right with other threads which lie across it. The stitch used here is a little more complicated than that shown in Fig. 84. In this variation, the thread has to be looped an extra time over the needle before carrying out the basic stitch.

There is another stitch which can be used for joining the end threads, and which is also very satisfactory: the point de reprise. This stitch can be practised using the method explained above.

The embryo is shown completed, and in colour, in Plate 5 facing page 48.

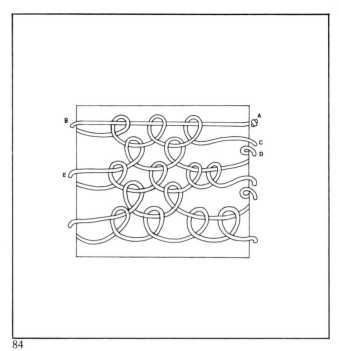

84

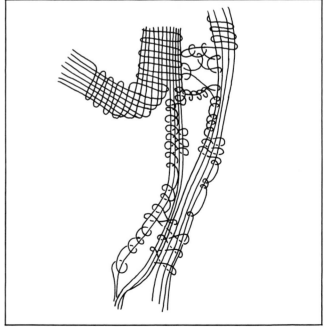

85

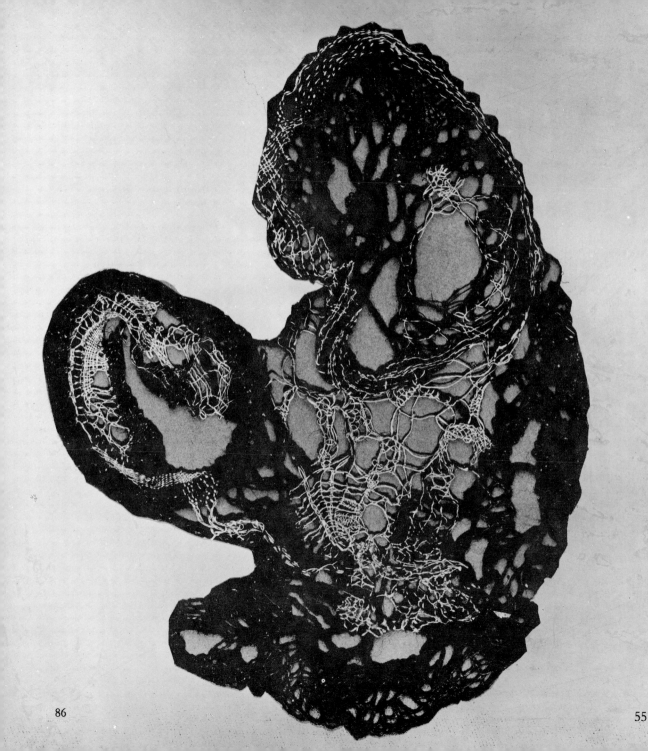

5. MOSS

This piece of bobbin lace work was done in five sections by four different people (three of whom had had only eight lessons). Plate 7 facing page 56 shows the final result.

The original subject was a magazine photograph of a piece of moss (Fig. 87). This photograph was traced, and the resultant drawing cut into five sections (Fig. 88). The choice of colour was guided by the natural colours of the moss in the photograph, but a special colour was selected for the central section.

The orange, olive green, and golden brown yarn was handspun sheep's wool which had been dyed in madder, sorrel, and heather respectively, while thin and thick rough single ply linen yarn was used for the green, brown, and golden yellow portions of the design.

The working plan is shown in Fig. 88. In Fig. 90 parts A, B, D, and E have already been finished and sewn together with slip stitch. Part C is also finished, and waiting to be sewn to the other sections. Fig. 89 shows the work with section C sewn in.

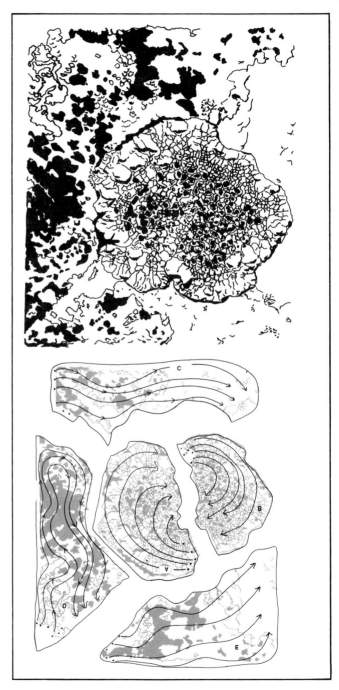

87

88

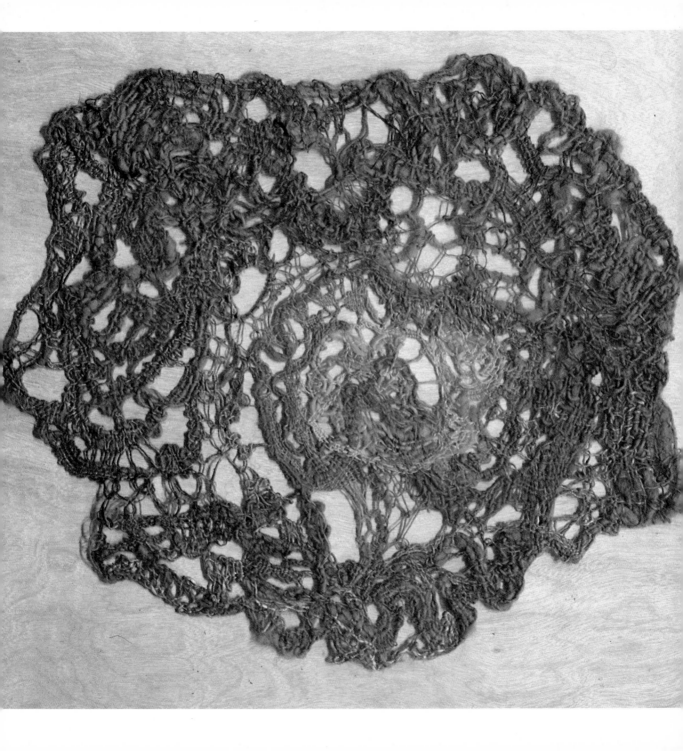

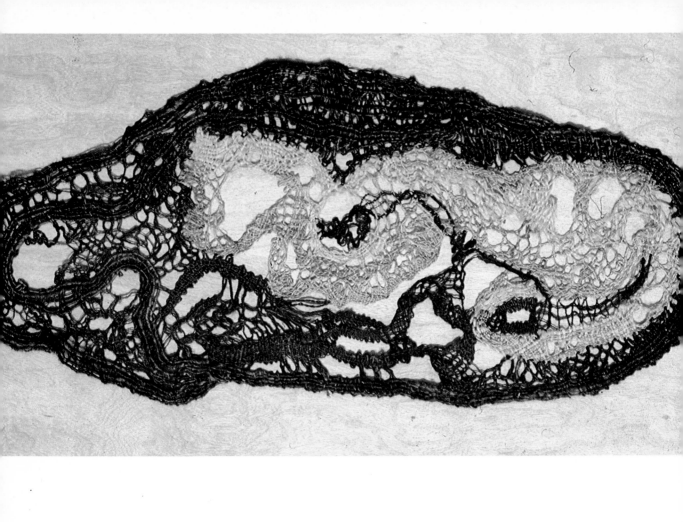

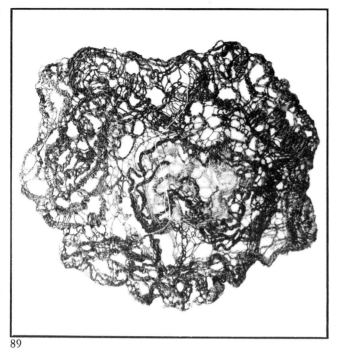

89

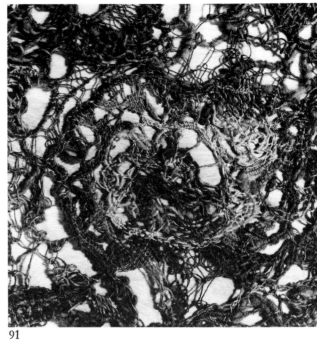

91

Here sections A and B can be seen in detail.

90

57

6. MUSSEL SHELL

This design is based on a barnacle-encrusted mussel shell, magnified about twenty times. The piece of lace it inspired is shown in Fig. 98, and in colour in Plate 8 preceding page 56.

The materials used were single and 2 ply linen yarn, partly handspun and home-dyed; and varying thicknesses of cotton and jute string. The drawing of the mussel shell is first enlarged; instructions for doing this will be found in Section 7.

The work is started at point A (see Fig. 99), to which are pinned bobbins wound with natural and blue-green linen yarn. The work is continued downwards. Then the pillow is turned round, and the left-hand side of the pattern completed. Some new bobbins are added on the way, and some threads are cut off; Fig. 94 shows the work in progress, and the tufts of loose threads which have still to be dealt with can be seen at the top left.

The lace is begun with about fifteen pairs of bobbins. The enlarged design is cut into three parts horizontally, and the work is started in the middle section. It may sometimes be necessary to push the pins holding the parts already completed right down into the cushion, since the bobbins have a tendency to catch on them; the completed sections should also be covered with a sheet of paper. The whole work will need to be removed from the pillow several times and pushed upwards to make more working space. Fig. 96 shows the left-hand section of the lace shell, and Fig. 97 the middle portion.

92

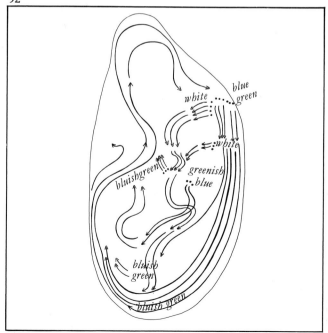

93

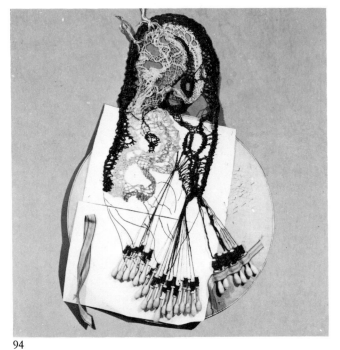

94

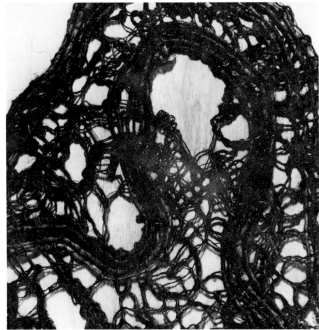

96

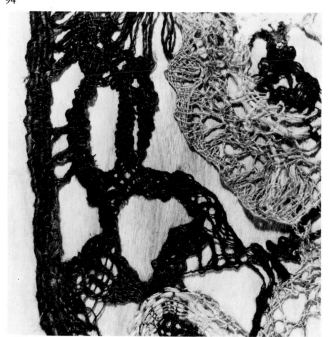

95

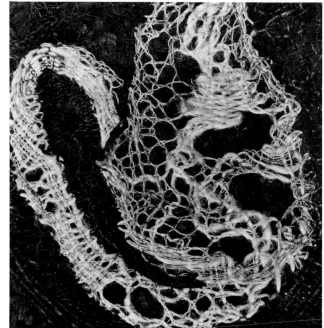

97

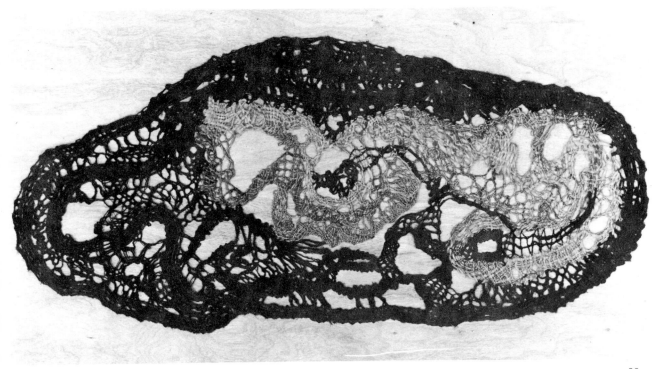

98

7. ENLARGING A DESIGN

In the 'Mussel shell' section it was mentioned that this design was enlarged. This is how it is done.

The shell is drawn on a sheet of paper measuring about 10 ins. × 20 ins. (24 cm. × 48 cm.), but the lace shell is intended to measure, say, 20 ins. × 40 ins. (48 cm. × 96 cm.). This means that the design has to be made twice as big. A series of horizontal and vertical lines is drawn on the paper at intervals of 2 ins. (4.8 cm.). The horizontal lines are each given a letter, while the vertical lines are given a number (Fig. 99).

On a piece of paper twice as big as the first sheet another series of horizontal and vertical lines is drawn, but this time at 4 inch (9.6 cm.) intervals. Each square of the original drawing can then easily be copied over twice as big. If the design was to be made three times as big as the original, each square would have had to be three times as big, and so on. In this way a design can be enlarged to practically any size, since it is possible to indicate exactly how a particular line should go on the enlarged drawing.

The points through which the lines of the enlarged design must run can now be marked out. The lower line of the shell, for instance, crosses point A7 and then passes a little way under half the line B7-8 towards the middle line C7-8, etc. Fig. 100 shows square B4-C4-B5-C5 of the enlarged drawing superimposed on a photograph of the corresponding part of the finished work. The enlarged design was in fact cut into three horizontally to make it easier for working.

8. MOUNTING LACE

One or two points about mounting lace might be welcome at this stage. A very fine effect can be created by pinning a piece of bobbin lace to a sheet of dark cork, using black pins which will be almost invisible. Another advantage is that the work will keep its shape perfectly.

Another method, apart from putting the lace in a conventional wooden or metal outer frame, is to nail it directly on to a wooden board, using the end threads if necessary; this last method makes subsequent framing, if desired, much easier.

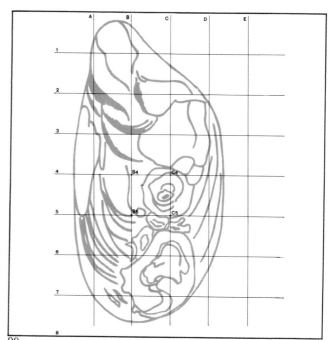

99

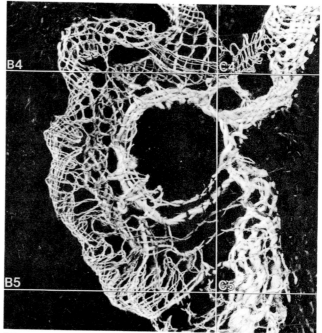

100

61

9. TREEBARK 1

Thick and thin rough linen yarn in a range of colours was used in this piece of lace, based on a piece of red-brown bark picked up in a wood. This is an example of work done all in one piece, starting at the top and finishing at the bottom. Fig. 101 shows the finished lace.

10. VEGETABLE SALAD

Fig. 104 shows a red cabbage and a pepper, cut into sections to show how beautiful they are inside, and how suitable they are as subjects for free bobbin lace. Two pieces of bark and an onion were added to make an attractive composition. This piece of work was done in separate parts, which were then knitted together.

The materials used were single and 2 ply linen yarn, buttonhole silk, and twisted cotton yarn. One or two uninteresting-looking sections were decorated with needle lace, using the end threads. The finished lace can be seen in Fig. 103, and a detail of the pepper in Fig. 102.

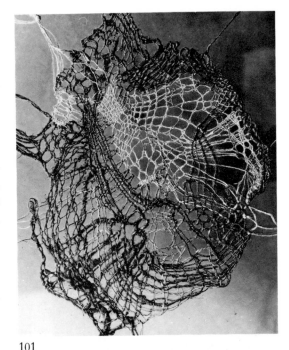

101

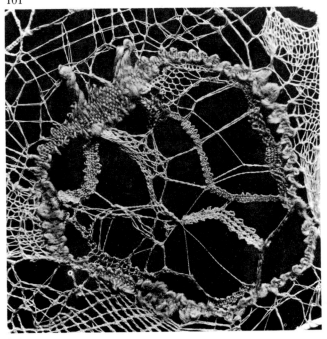

102

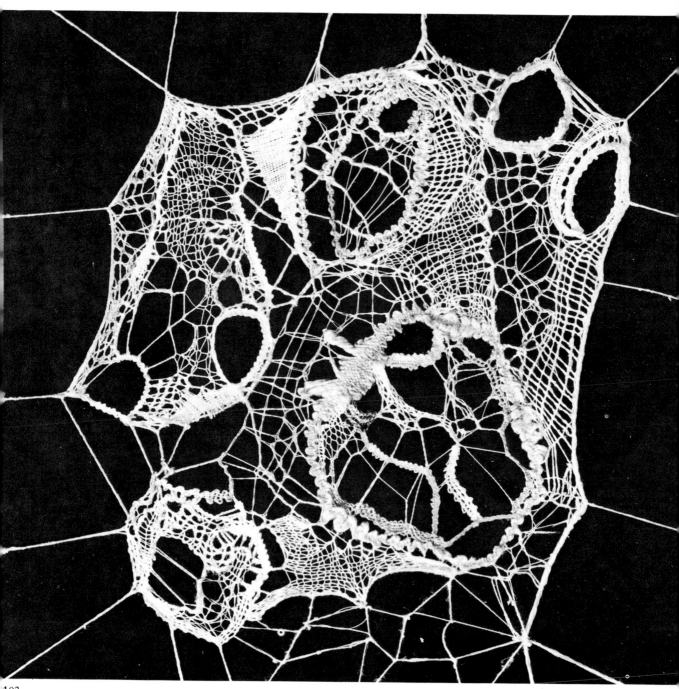

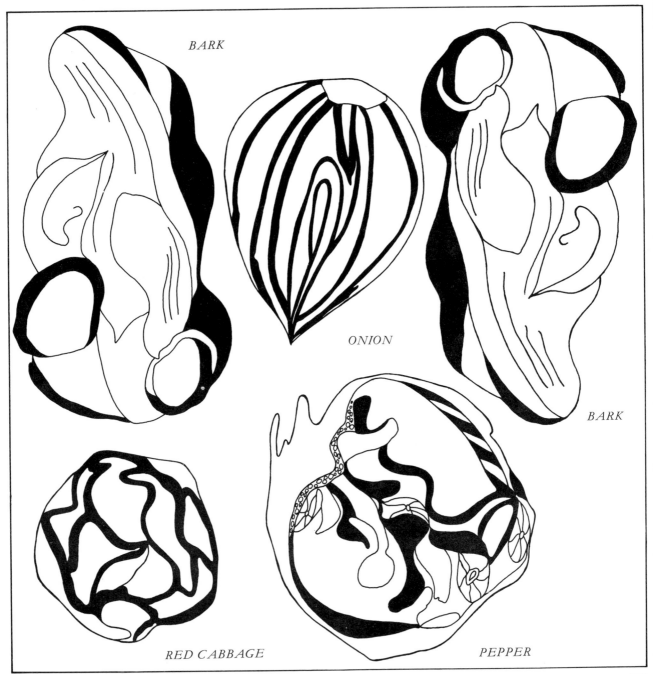

BARK

ONION

BARK

RED CABBAGE

PEPPER

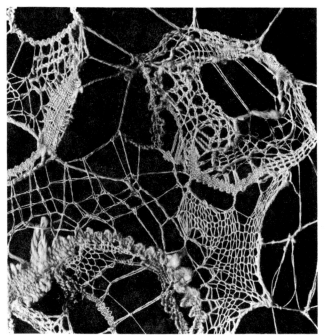

105

9. TREEBARK 2

This is a piece of the bark that accompanied the vegetables in the previous section, but enlarged (see Section 7). Again, single and 2 ply linen yarn and cotton were used, this time in a range of greens and blue-greens.

The lower and left-hand sections are done as a whole. The middle section is then knitted, and the combined sections pinned on to the pillow. The upper section is started by attaching bobbins to the knitted section as described in the 'Thorn apple' design. Finally, the whole work was mounted in a metal frame (see Section 8), and secured with the end threads.

The finished work can be seen in Fig. 108. Figs. 106 and 107 show two details of the work. Fig. 107 shows how the work was done in a circular motion, with the running pair constantly picking up loops on the other side.

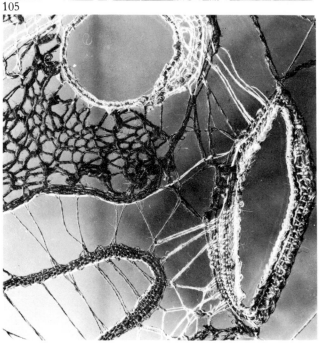

106

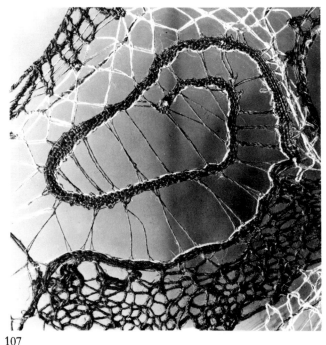

107

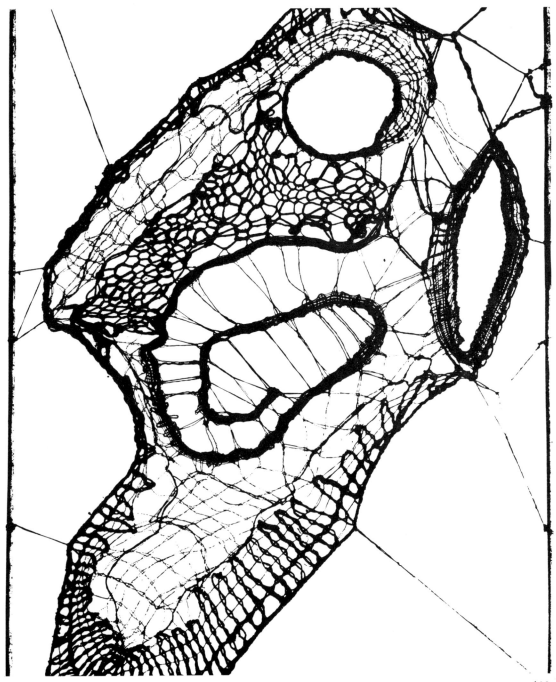

10. DANCING FIGURES

These whimsical little dancing creatures are just a flight of fancy, but a rather attractive one.

The knitted parts are made first, following a large pattern pinned to a sheet of cork measuring 30 ins. × 60 ins. (72 cm. × 144 cm.); Fig. 109 is a drawing of the design. These sections are then mounted on the drawing with pins, and bobbins are attached at those points of the figure's body to be in bobbin lace. The upper section is worked in a circle, which is then hitched on to the finished section by the looping technique already described in the 'Thorn apple' design.

Figs. 110 and 111 show details of the middle and lower sections of the figure.

The upper, middle, and lower sections are linked together by a long strip of bobbin lace, the end threads tidied up and the whole work placed in a wooden frame measuring 30 ins. × 60 ins. (72 cm. × 144 cm.) (see Plate 3 facing page 40 and Fig. 112). The materials used are single and 2 ply wool, partly handspun; single and 2 ply linen thread; and sisal string. The woollen threads are dyed orange with madder.

109

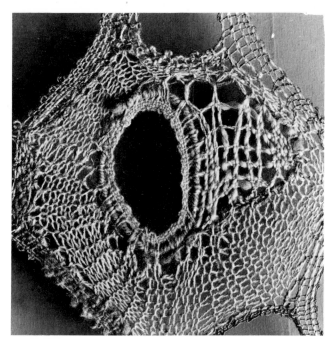

110

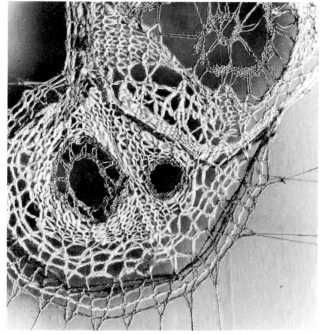

111

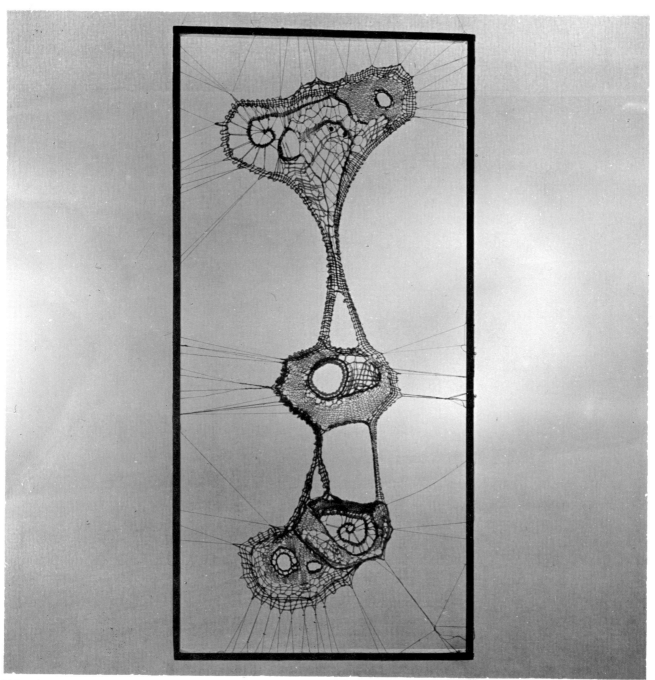

Suppliers

GREAT BRITAIN

Mace & Nairn, 89 Crane St., Salisbury, Wilts., SP1 2PY sell bobbins, linen yarn, and pins.

The Needlewoman Shop, 146 Regent St., London W1 sell bobbins, and cotton and linen yarn.

Christine Riley, 53 Barclay St., Stonehaven, Kincardineshire, AB3 2AR sell bobbins, and cotton yarn.

Woollen yarn is readily obtainable from specialist yarn shops, knitting wool shops, and department stores in Great Britain and the United States.

Chemical dyes can be bought from craft shops and department stores.

UNITED STATES

Some Place, 2990 Adeline St., Berkeley, Calif. 94703 sell a basic bobbin lace kit.

Berga/Ullman, Box 831, Ossining, New York, N.Y. 10562 sell a traditional Swedish padded lace pillow, bobbins, etc.

Yarn Center, 866 Avenue of the Americas, New York, N.Y. sell a wide variety of yarns.

Robin & Russ Handweavers, 533 North Adams Street, McMinniville, Oregon 97128 sell a wide variety of yarns.

Merribee Needlecraft Company, 2904 West Lancaster, Fort Worth, Texas 76107 sell yarns by mail order; also have a number of retail shops.

Frederick J. Fawcett, Inc., 129 South Street, Boston, Mass. 02111 sell all kinds of linen yarn.

SYMBOLS FOR BOBBIN LACE STITCHES USED IN THIS BOOK

☐ cloth stitch

⊡ double cloth stitch

△ gauze stitch

▲ rose-net stitch (double gauze stitch)

• pin

× turning

× × turning twice

⧖ plait or braiding

✕ passing a thick thread to the right

✕ passing a thick thread to the left

≡ point de reprise

⇄ direction in which the row is being worked (this will be followed by a symbol indicating the relevant stitch).

70

Books of related interest from Van Nostrand Reinhold

Lace

TRADITIONAL LACE MAKING
Johanson

NEW DESIGNS IN LACE MAKING
Malmberg & Thorlin

TATTING: PATTERNS AND DESIGNS
Blomqvist & Persson

TATTING
Auld
(published by Van Nostrand Reinhold
in the United States,
and by David and Charles in Great Britain)

Related crafts

DRAWN THREADWORK
Melen

KNOTTING AND NETTING:
THE ART OF FILET WORK
Melen

MACRAME: THE ART OF CREATIVE KNOTTING
Harvey

COLOR AND DESIGN IN MACRAME
Harvey

PRACTICAL MODERN CROCHET
Lind

Spinning and dyeing

SPINNING AND DYEING THE NATURAL WAY
Castino & Pickens
(published by Van Nostrand Reinhold
in the United States,
and by Evans Brothers Ltd. in Great Britain)

HANDSPINNING
Fannin

DYES FROM PLANTS
Robertson

CARDING, SPINNING, DYEING
Hoppe & Edberg